Comeback Wolves

Comeback Wolves

Western Writers Welcome the Wolf Home

Edited by Gary Wockner
Gregory McNamee
SueEllen Campbell

Foreword by Congressman Mark Udall

Johnson Books
BOULDER

Published by Johnson Books, a subsidiary of Big Earth Publishing,
3005 Center Green Drive, Suite 220, Boulder, Colorado 80301. www.johnsonbooks.com

Pattiann Rogers, Song of the World Becoming: New and Collected Poems, 1981–2001
(Minneapolis: Milkweed Editions, 2001). Copyright © 2001 by Pattiann Rogers.
Reprinted with permission of the author and Milkweed Editions, www.milkweed.org.

Cover design by Erika Echols
Cover photograph by hargreavesphoto.com
Wolf paw illustration by Elizabeth Biesiot

9 8 7 6 5 4 3 2 1

Library of Congress Cataloging-in-Publication Data
Comeback wolves: western writers welcome the wolf home / edited by Gary
Wockner, Gregory McNamee, and SueEllen Campbell.
       p. cm.
     ISBN 1-55566-365-6
     1. Wolves—West (U.S.) 2. Wolves—Psychological aspects. 3. Human-animal
relationships. 4. Wolves—Poetry. I. Wockner, Gary. II. McNamee, Gregory. III.
Campbell, SueEllen.
   QL737.C22C625 2005
   599.773'0978—dc22   2005018964

Printed in the United States of America

Contents

Becoming Wolf

Landscapes with Wolves

Resources

Foreword

by Congressman Mark Udall

Very few people have experienced the call of the wolf in the wild. It used to be a part of the allure of the outdoors, symbolizing in an instant the sense of open space, limitless vistas, brilliant blue skies, recuperative solitude, and the rugged wildness that inheres in the landscape of the American West. However, because wolves were feared as threats to ranching livelihoods, wolf populations dwindled dramatically in the nineteenth and twentieth centuries. Ultimately, wolves were exterminated by the federal government across almost all of the western United States.

But times have changed, and so has the fate of the wolf.

In 1995, the Clinton administration brought back wolves to the Greater Yellowstone ecosystem, where they once lived in large numbers. Since then, wolves are making a comeback, and their range is growing. The body of one Yellowstone wolf (dispersed from Northwest Wyoming) was found—killed by an automobile on June 7, 2004, along Interstate 70 near Idaho Springs, Colorado—almost five hundred miles south of Yellowstone.

This incident has been cause for celebration in some circles—not because of the wolf's death, but as evidence that wolves are returning to the West. It also has created concern among ranchers and rural communities as wandering wolves resurrect the specter of economic competition. With this possible (some say eventual) return of the wolf, we must be careful not to re-create the situations that caused conflicts between wolves and humans when the West was first being settled. "Management" and "sustainability" are the key concepts that should guide us through this new era.

As we begin managing for wolves, it is important to remember that wolves and other predators were part of the historic ecological balance that once existed across America's landscapes. The fact that wolves are now thriving in some areas underscores that they can continue to fill this important ecological niche. Deer and elk—wolves' primary source of food—are abundant in Colorado and the Rocky Mountain West. The ecological role of the wolf is underscored by research demonstrating that since the species was reintroduced in the Yellowstone, willows and aspen also are returning, songbirds not seen in the park for generations have come back, elk are again behaving like wild elk and are no longer devastating vegetation in riparian areas, and coyote populations have been reduced.

Most people who are receptive to seeing wolves again fulfilling these ecological functions are equally reluctant to permit wolves to cause harm to our region's already hard-pressed farmers and ranchers. Most of these rural landowners are stalwart conservationists who love, respect, and protect the land. In our management activities, we need to find a sustainable way for humans and wolves to coexist. Committees and task forces in Colorado and other states are looking into this very issue, their work hurried along by the discovery of the wolf along I-70. Programs like the two created by Defenders of Wildlife—the Wolf Compensation Trust and the Proactive Carnivore Conservation Fund—which compensate ranchers for livestock losses to predators and help share techniques to avoid further losses, are important contributions to this effort.

With these collaborative programs among landowners, conservation groups, and government agencies, the threats from wolves can be minimized and our management can be sustainable. If we learn to alter our behavior slightly, it is likely that wolves will focus on their native prey—deer and elk—and largely leave livestock alone. Programs that help educate the public are also an important part of sustainable and balanced management. Some people fear that wolves are a threat to human life, and good education programs can reduce these fears. I am not an expert on wolf behavior, but history has shown that wolves are rarely human killers. In fact, there have been no documented human kills in the lower 48 states.

All of this is by way of saying that we must proceed with caution when it comes to wolves, and we need to be respectful of their power, but not succumb to irrational prejudices and fears. So let's leave the mythical and fairy-tale depictions of wolves in stories like "Little Red Riding Hood" to literature and fiction, and place our policy making in the real world.

Wolves do indeed evoke strong passions. These passions are represented in the following pages by some of the West's most notable writers and poets. All of the pieces here come from people with a deep appreciation of the West and a special love for the lore of the wolf. They speak from the heart about mysteries and experiences that should matter to all of us who care about the future of our planet.

I have had the good fortune to travel through much of the West. I grew up in Arizona, and as a child I traveled extensively with my family around desert and mountain landscapes. Later, my experiences teaching with the Colorado Outward Bound School reinforced my deep love for this part of our country. Heading Colorado Outward Bound, in particular, was a formative experience for me. Outward Bound utilizes the challenges of outdoor life to build both inner strength and the skills of collaborative leadership. To stretch a metaphor to fit the occasion, students in Outward Bound are like wolves in the pack—they learn individual survival skills while at the same time learning the value of a larger community. Now, as a member of Congress, I hesitate to draw too many favorable comparisons between my current position and with Outward Bound or with the wolf pack, but my love of the West continues.

I have hiked, skied, climbed, kayaked, rafted, and biked many places where wolves once roamed and could again thrive. Once, while skiing through the Brooks Range in Alaska, my companions and I sighted a wolf along a ridge. Being in such a remote location—the closest town was more than three hundred miles away—the sight of this wolf produced exhilaration tinged with apprehension. On another occasion, I was equally thrilled when I thought I spotted a wolf while hiking in the Wallowa Mountains in Oregon. In both cases, after the excitement of the encounters had subsided, I felt fortunate to have the opportunity to see wolves in their natural habitat, and I reflected on how much wolves exemplify the wilderness experience.

I believe that the human soul is stirred when a hawk's high-pitched chirp echoes down a river canyon, when the crack of horn-butting Rocky Mountain bighorn sheep sounds off the granite walls of a high mountain valley, or when trout ripple the surface of a still lake.

The call of a wolf used to evoke similar respect for our natural world. We can experience that again, and we need not fear the wolf's return. It can remind us of the West as it once was and as we hope to see it become, a West where opportunities are endless, where the human spirit can be uplifted and rejuvenated, and where human development and habitation can coexist with nature in its wildest forms.

With the help and support of many people—including the authors here—we can bring back that unique sense of wonder, awe, and respect that wolves create. I know you will enjoy the selections here and will find wonder in these pages. But most of all, I hope you will develop a deeper appreciation of nature and find more time to get out, experience the many things it has to offer, and help protect it, too.

Introduction

Wolves have been missing from Colorado and the Southern Rocky Mountains for a very long time, hunted out over the years, driven into exile and to near-extinction. But they are on their way back, one way or another, after their long absence. This book, a collection of essays and poems from some of the region's best-known writers, celebrates their return.

The wolves in these pages howl, lope, swim, kill sheep, and cull herds of cattle and wild elk and deer. They appear in dreams and waking apparitions. They terrify and guard us. They hide from us. Some are legendary; others live in movies and souvenir shops. They dress up in human guise, shop, play soccer, stroll down urban streets. Some of them are flesh-and-blood animals, but more are imagined—for, after all, few people have actually seen these storied animals.

Above all, this book is full of wild and hoped-for wolves.

The contributors to it are nature and science writers, novelists, poets, journalists, activists, and biologists. We are members of ranch families, teachers, parents, wildlife watchers, rural, small town, and city folks. Nearly all of us live or have lived in the Southern Rockies, mostly in Colorado, a few in Arizona, New Mexico, and Utah. More than a few of us are native to these places, with families whose roots here are deep.

In these pages we explore the spaces that separate and connect action—social, environmental, scientific, political—with imagination and desire. We explore, remember, think, rant, chant, and yearn. We paint pictures and tell stories. We write from our hearts, minds, and passions.

∼

This book owes its genesis to the convergence of several forces in the late spring of 2004. By early June of that year, it seemed likely that the U.S. Fish and Wildlife Service might, within the next few years, reintroduce wolves into Colorado, as they have been reintroduced to Wyoming, Idaho, New Mexico, and Arizona. Rocky Mountain National Park was considering wolves as one possible way to control elk populations. And the Colorado Division of Wildlife had appointed a Wolf Management Plan Working Group—conservationists, ranchers, biologists, county commissioners, and hunters brought together to write a plan for the eventual migration, and perhaps reintroduction, of wolves into Colorado.

Then a gray wolf was found dead on I-70 near Idaho Springs, hit by a car or truck. She was "Wolf 293F"—a two-year-old female from the Swan Lake pack centered near Mammoth Hot Springs in the northwest corner of Wyoming. Sometime after mid-January, in search of a mate and territory for her own new pack, she traveled more than four hundred miles southeast through Wyoming and about a third of Colorado, surviving, apparently, on deer. No one knows her whole story, of course, but there are enough fragments to feed the imagination, and so, practically overnight, for many Coloradans, she became a symbol of her species' possible return. As you will see, she appears here and there in these pages, and it is she to whom we have dedicated this book.

Wolves once roamed widely in Colorado. Although no one counted them during the height of westward expansion, some observers at the time suggested that up to 39,000 may have lived here in the mid-1800s. In 1869, the state enacted a wolf bounty and over the next sixty years paid thousands of bounties for pelts. By the end of the century, something between one thousand and thirteen thousand wolves still lived here. By the late 1930s, wolves had become extremely rare in Colorado, and while sources vary on the date of the last wolf killing—and while nobody can know for sure when the very last one vanished—by the late 1940s, they were almost surely gone.

Wolves were exterminated in Colorado, as they were throughout the United States, for three main reasons. Ranchers and farmers saw them as relentless killers of livestock, as threats to their livelihood. Wildlife managers felt, similarly, that wolves killed too many deer, elk, antelope, and moose; if wolves were gone, they thought, these herds would flourish. And, inheriting a long cultural tradition from Europe, wolves were widely seen as symbols of wild nature's savagery, of what European-American settlers needed to subdue as they expanded across the continent.

Times and attitudes have changed, for the most part. Because it is a simple fact that wolves do sometimes kill and eat sheep and cows, most of the current debate about wolves and wolf reintroduction across the West and Colorado still focuses on this fact and what to do about it. In the western

United States in 2004, the environmental organization Defenders of Wildlife paid $139,000 to livestock producers for 558 wolf-killed sheep, cows, and a few other domesticated animals—far fewer than the thousands of domesticated animals killed by coyotes and feral dogs in the same areas. Much is being done around the West not just to pay ranchers for animals killed by wolves but also to minimize conflicts by keeping wolves and livestock separate.

No such problems linger for wildlife managers, who now see wolves as integral parts of natural systems, as creatures whose absence causes more harm than good. In ecosystems where wolves are present, such as Isle Royale and now Yellowstone, the interaction of predator and prey has been teaching both scientists and the public about the importance of these naturally regulating systems.

Perhaps most important, we no longer think of wild nature and its inhabitants as savage forces to subdue, but rather as treasures to protect and nurture. And so our ideas about wolves are changing. The Big Bad Wolf who threatens to blow our houses down is giving way to a shimmering array of new images: the benevolent parent with squirming pups, the loner howling at the moon, the sunlit runners in a spray of flying snow. Public opinion polls report that nearly seventy percent of Coloradans support wolf reintroduction. That wolves deserve another chance is now the norm of thinking throughout the West, as elsewhere in the United States.

And so this is a book not about wolf biology or the economics of ranching or the policy options for wolf population management, though some of these essays and poems touch on some of these things. Instead, it is about the new ways we are finding to understand wolves—to think about them, imagine them, and welcome them home.

The idea for *Comeback Wolves* began with Gary Wockner, ecologist, writer, and member of the Colorado Wolf Working Group, who wanted to create a space for writers in Colorado and the Southwest to add their voices to the conversations among politicians, ranchers, biologists, wildlife managers, and the public. Before long, nature writer and literary scholar SueEllen Campbell and freelance journalist and author Gregory McNamee had signed on as coeditors. Emails flew around the West—invitations to contribute, deadlines set for the autumn equinox, conversations of many kinds. We invited dozens of the West's best and most prolific writers—authors of more than 250 books, collectively, on nature and environmental issues, frequent contributors to *Orion, Sierra, High Country News, Mountain Gazette,* and many other magazines and journals both environmental and literary. More than a few hesitated because they'd never seen a wild wolf: one of the most commonly seen creatures on the continent during the country's westward expansion had escaped the eyes of many of the West's leading writers and poets. Yet again and again, these writers said they felt honored to have the chance to speak about, and perhaps for, these animals. And then they wrote something new, an essay or a poem composed just for this book.

Each of us considers a part of the big picture, a part of the puzzle. Taken together, our diverse contributions suggest the shape and colors of what is a complex landscape of hope, concern, restitution, and wildness.

We have divided the contents into five parts, each exploring one major subset of our topic. Within these parts, individual pieces speak to each other, amplify or complement or oppose each other. Other divisions and other orders would have been equally possible, and we know you will discover your own threads of continuity and conversation. Each section title is drawn from one of its following essays or poems and suggests the theme that holds the section together.

The first section, "Invocations to Return the Wolf," introduces the major themes and motifs of the book. The second section, "A Howling from the Belly," focuses on the strong passions this animal provokes, on all the fear, hope, and wildness the wolf's howl suggests to those who hear it. The third section, "The Voltage of Legends," explores some of the many stories people have told themselves about wolves and the images we have inherited through our myths and language. The fourth section, "Becoming Wolf," considers our own human kinship with these other living creatures. Finally, the fifth section, "Landscapes with Wolves," imagines what it will be like to live in a place where wolves have always belonged and to which they will finally return.

∽

Because we agree with Edward Abbey that "sentiment without action is the ruin of the soul," we have taken several steps to give this book a role in the realm of actions as well as in that of ideas and emotions.

First, the initial printing will include a few hundred copies that we will distribute to Colorado legislators and county commissioners as well as the relevant decision makers in the state and federal government. Second, all contributors have agreed to donate all royalties from this book to the Defenders of Wildlife's Proactive Carnivore Conservation Fund, which we believe to be the best thing going to protect wolves and other carnivores while also preserving ranches and the open landscapes they require. You can find out more about this fund at the end of the book, and we will report on it and other relevant news about wolf reintroduction at our web site, www.comebackwolves.com. And finally, again at the end of the book, we offer links to all the organizations in the Intermountain West that are working to restore wolves. Action, indeed, is needed.

Nature is reeducating us. The wolf is our teacher. We are honored to help.

Gary Wockner
Gregory McNamee
SueEllen Campbell

For Wolf 293F

Invocations to Return the Wolf

The poems and essays in this opening section introduce many of the issues, themes, and motifs that will follow throughout the book: our culture's lingering fears and hatreds; our need to replace our more destructive myths with new knowledge, new images, and new ways of thinking; the quest to see these storied animals so many of us have undertaken; the ecological healing that wolves can create; and our desire for their return to their ancestral homes in Colorado and the Southern Rocky Mountains.

Evan Oakley

Evan Oakley teaches at Aims Community College in Loveland, Colorado. His poetry has appeared in various places including the North American Review. For many years, he codirected the annual "Poets in the Park," which featured Pulitzer Prize winners, a poet laureate of the United States, and other poets of national standing. Contemplating myths and facts, extinction and wildness, Oakley speaks directly to the wolf, the "Unlikely beast," and asks of it that we might "learn / just what you are."

Invocation to Return the Wolf

You're not like the other beasts,
not in myth, not in fact,
your by no means certain feasts
leave little intact,
not entrails, not composure:
there you are, in a rancher's dreams,
loping through the enclosure,
crossing the frozen streams
to bring carnage on the village.
More likely, you'd prefer a host
of mice, snuffed up from tillage,
a rotting fawn, at most,
some less than nimble elk.
Unlike the other beasts,
your eyes, a mythic yeast,
rise in dreams; at your howl
binoculars range west & east;
moods grow foul,
they'd kill you in their dreams,
with snares in the enclosures,
with purchased screams

from legislators, with censures
from the village lawyers.
They'd return your status
to *absent*. They'd like the voyeurs
at the zoo to contemplate a hiatus
from which you will not return.
Wild one, a wild day has come,
the kind you'd like, maybe. Some
yearn to see you haunt the timber,
some to burn your heart to char.
Unlikely beast: let us learn
just what you are.

SueEllen Campbell

SueEllen Campbell teaches nature and environmental literature at Colorado State University. Her books include Even Mountains Vanish: Searching for Solace in an Age of Extinction *and* Bringing the Mountain Home. *In this essay she looks for wolves in books, souvenir shops, and North America's wildlands; moving gradually closer to her Colorado home, she watches these animals move from myth into reality.*

Looking for Wolves

When my great-great-grandparents moved to Colorado in 1872, they probably feared the wolves they saw. Perhaps, when as a young mother she lived on a farm, my great-grandmother Bessie shot one. Even my grandmother Elizabeth, who liked to hike and ride in the mountains, might one day have seen a wild wolf in the distance, a shadow of gray slipping among aspen trunks. Though both Bessie and Elizabeth lived until I was nearly thirty, and though I saw them often, it never occurred to me to ask either of them about these animals: wolves seemed so long and impossibly gone.

Instead, in the twenty or so years since my grandmothers died, I've read about wolves. I started with books by Barry Lopez and Aldo Leopold, then buried myself in the narratives of Arctic travelers. Later, I read Charles Bergman's work, Cormac McCarthy's novels, and Farley Mowat's classic *Never Cry Wolf.* From these books I learned that while sometimes we allow wild wolves in the far north to live, we have wanted the rest to die.

For a long time now I've been haunted by Leopold's image of a species being hunted toward extinction, one life at a time—how he saw a single wolf shake herself out of white water and join a group of grown pups in a flurry of playful welcome, how he and his companions emptied their rifles into the "mêlée of wagging tails," and finally, how he watched her die, this one old wolf, watched "a fierce green fire dying in her eyes."

September 1994, and I'm in Minnesota's Boundary Waters, some twelve hundred road miles from my home in northern Colorado. I've gone to considerable trouble to get here, but three days of frigid rain, slick portages, pinched nerves, and nothing but mist, moss, and muck to look at have buried my spirits. Early on the fourth day, I hear a ghostly howl. Is it a coyote? I don't think so—I hear coyotes often at home, usually as I'm waiting to fall asleep, and this sound is different, its rhythm longer, its tone maybe deeper. I know that here it might possibly be—and so, reckoning by imagination and desire, I resolve that it must be—a distant wolf, out there somewhere in the misty, tangled forest, invisible as if in a fairy tale that somehow includes me. As faint as it is, this voice out of myth and history, this voice I've really never thought I'd hear, snaps me out of my misery and back into a landscape full of life: the sun burns through, a moose crashes forward, a beaver slaps, loons cry.

∿

July 1998, Bathurst Inlet, Canadian Arctic, almost four hundred air miles beyond the last road. I'm in the bow of a canoe paddling south, away from the pale peach glow where in an hour or so the sun will dip briefly out of sight. Calm air, glassy water. For days now I've felt as though I were floating in some liminal space of dreamy alertness, and tonight the enchantment is strong, the sting of mosquitoes around my head and the slightly skewed pull of the canoe my only links to the mundane. We're looking for the foxes we've heard have a den upstream. I doubt we'll succeed, but I don't care—just being here is marvelous.

Do I expect—or even hope—to see a wolf? No. Even here, in this vast spare land where I suppose they might live, I don't quite believe in them, and I certainly don't think I'll ever see one.

But that's what appears, not fifty yards ahead on the bank to our right. It seems to have materialized out of nothing, out of blue air, flowering tundra, the midnight sun. It is white, lean, leggy, and side-lit. For one hypnotic moment, it looks at us and we gaze back. It glows like an apparition of light, of magic, of some other kind of reality.

∿

May 2000, Fairbanks, nearly four thousand road miles from home. I'm in the living room of the Honors Program house on the University of Alaska campus, teaching a summer course on the literature of wildness with my friend Walter Isle. We've read an essay about wolf trapping by local writer Sherry Simpson, and today she is visiting our class. Her essay is terrific—

thoughtful, troubling, provocative, and complicated—but what really gets our attention is the wolfskin she's brought. She clearly wants us all to handle it, in a complex gesture of respect on her part and ours.

This wolf died for the allure of her skin. And there's no denying its jet and silver beauty—even indoors, even lying heavy, hot, and inert in my lap. The fur is so thick that as I stroke it, my fingers disappear.

I've heard human skin described as our largest organ, and now I'm holding the empty skin of a dead wolf. Part of an animal's body is here in my hands. What would it be like, I wonder, to hold a wolf's heart or its brain, its lungs or its leg muscles? I suppose they too might suggest the power of this animal, who once howled in the early morning, once tangled with others in a flurry of welcome, once walked along a creek bank in the midnight sun. I could try to imagine a life for her, I know, but what I really want—to restore her to her own—is impossible. It would require a miracle.

〜

Finally I start looking for wolves in the Lamar Valley of Yellowstone, where I know they've been reintroduced—not too far from home now, two easy days in a car. One day my husband, John, and I arrive at the edge of the valley just as dusk becomes dark, too late after a day's driving and roadside dawdling, with no time to linger overnight. Another time we arrive at midday, with no wild animals about and few people, just a researcher tracking coyotes as their local population plummets under the pressure of the wolves.

So instead I survey the gift shops at nearby Mammoth Hot Springs. Here the choice among wolfish curios is impressive, though most items fall between moderate and extreme on my SS&T scale—Schmaltz, Schlock, and Tackiness.

I find wolves, and parts of wolves, on the usual T-shirts, sweatshirts, refrigerator magnets, mugs, and postcards. Key chains, playing cards, pins. A puppet and a furry wolf-head hat, two sizes of stuffed animals. Picture frames and a howling Christmas tree ornament. A candle, also howling, its wick rising from the upturned mouth. A cedar box decorated with a full moon and a wolf, howling, of course, with a puff of vapor above its mouth. Coasters and placemats. Hammered copper and scorched wood plaques.

Lots of statues—wolf heads rising out of whole wolf bodies in various combinations and arrangements. A snowless snowglobe holding a wolf head, resting on a base encircled by whole wolves. This last may be my favorite; if it were smaller, and if it had snow, I'd think about buying it to sit on my kitchen windowsill next to my elk-with-gold-flake-snow and flamingoes-with-iridescent-snow globes. My SS&T winners are certainly the two greeting cards on "tree-free paper," each sporting a scantily clad Indian maiden. One holds a giant moon in front of which a wolf howls on a cliff. The other seems to be dreaming of wolves, whose heads and front legs emerge from a wintry sky.

What's all this about? I think about this question for a long ti me, listen to all the voices in my head deliver their judgments, argue it out. The critic in me, and its twin, the cynic: *bad taste, sloppy sentimentalism, money, waste.* The part of me that remembers how to play: *funny and harmless.* The wilderness purist in me has a lot to say: *paltry substitutes for reality . . . how about some pictures of wolves tearing flesh from a bison carcass or killing a baby elk or a lamb or a pet dog? . . . those poor animals, loaded down with such a heavy weight of symbolism they never chose and know nothing about . . . and what's with the disembodied heads and wolves with only their front legs?*

But another more generous part of me likes it all, even the SS&T champions. If the debate about wolves is largely about images, as I think it is, then at least these howling candles and dreaming maidens aren't likely to incite hatred or slaughter or the desire to exterminate a species. There are far worse things to think about wolves than that they are beautiful, that they sing, that they are playful and familial, that they move between our world and some other realm of dreams and magic, that they represent power, freedom, survival, wildness. Plus all these curios can't possibly be aimed at government biologists and professional environmentalists: they're for the rest of us, the millions of ordinary people who visit this park every year. It heartens me that so many of us want to be reminded of these animals, whatever it is that they mean to us, that we want somehow to take them home.

$\sim$

July–August 2004. I return to the Lamar Valley for my third and fourth attempts to see a wolf here, first with John, then with my friend Mary Lea. This time the park is full of animals. With four whole days to spend in patient looking, we see antelope, buffalo, elk, black bears, and bighorns; a badger (my first), coyotes, a fox; eagles and osprey; a grizzly bear and— yes!—wolves.

And this time I find myself part of a wolf-watching community.

Some thirty people share a perch up a steep hill with me, along with eight spotting scopes, fifteen pairs of binoculars, two walkie-talkies, who knows how many cameras. Near a parking lot, I count fifty other people, one radio signal receiver, and ten scopes.

Some of these folks, I learn, come here to watch every summer, some for weeks, even months, at a time. They know the wolves by name, and they follow their unfolding stories: 42F, Druid Peak alpha female dead since early this year, obituaries across the nation; 21M, alpha male feared dead in July, body found in August; 286F, new alpha female; 253M presumptive but contested heir to 21M's position. I'm surprised and delighted at how captivated these people are by these wolves, how undeterred by the gesture of scientific objectivity embedded in their numerical names, how curious and passionate and respectful they are about the individual animals and the species recovery they are enacting. And so I learn quickly to recognize the most experienced and generous watchers, and I track these trackers, listen to them, peer through their scopes, learn from them how to find what I'm looking for.

We all talk to each other with raised arms and gestures, with a basic vocabulary of orientation: *See that fat bush in the middle of the field? The three tall pines behind it? The mound just to their left? Follow the line of that mound further to the left, halfway to that steep bank. See?* We shout to the deafer watchers, stoop low for the shortest, pantomime when English doesn't work. All the conversation here seems to be practical, none of it philosophical or spiritual. When one man says he quit his job and moved west so he could spend more time watching wolves, the listeners just nod and smile, and nobody asks him why. When a wolf appears, our language expands to include exclamations—*Awesome! Cool! Wow! Isn't that great!*—ordinary, trite words, more reflexes than thoughts, but adequate, somehow, to the immediacy of the moment.

Mary Lea has brought her brand-new scope—and mounts it backward on its tripod out of excitement at her first wolf sighting. Because she's fresh from her shopping research, I ask her to estimate the cost of the optical equipment we're seeing around us: an average of a thousand dollars for a spotting scope, she guesses, and maybe three hundred for binoculars. And the cameras, the airfares and car rentals and gasoline, the motels and campground fees, the meals? The vacation time saved up and spent here, the long hours cooped in cars and cramped airplane seats? This heartens me, too: how hard we'll work, how much we'll invest, coming together from all over the world, just to see these animals in the flesh.

The first wolves I see are wondrous. The rest—for we see at least seven different wolves on six occasions—are something else and better, something I can't quite articulate.

This is the first: Someone points out two black dots across the river on a small knoll. Through my binoculars I watch as one dot stands up, stretches into a body, head, and legs, then, lying back down, contracts again to a dot. Maybe it's silly to feel so excited about this sight, a pair of wolf dots in the distance, but I'm not the only one exclaiming: this is an adult pleasure, one that depends on our knowledge of history. Those dots are here, where they haven't been for decades, where once we'd erased them all, and we're seeing them with our own eyes. For us, it is the simple fact that matters—there are wolves in this valley, right now.

Another: I help a couple from Italy spot three wolves on a hillside just above the road. The two black ones are easier to see than the gray one, which disappears into the sagebrush except when it moves. Every minute or so one of them stands up, moves a few steps, lies back down, maybe shifting its view, maybe hoping for softer bedding. They're just lazing around; staring through our binoculars, we watchers are working harder than the wolves are. Suddenly, no transition, the two blacks are running fast, long legs stretching into speed, grace, and power, out of sight before we quite register what's happening. *Bellissimo!* exclaims the man at my side. *Bellissimo!*

And a third: Six wolves drop down the ridge to the north, cross the road, and wander around the valley for an hour or more in the chilly early morning. Two lope along a low ridge, disappear in the grass. Two pop out from behind some trees, drop over a cutbank out of sight. One walks to the river's edge, then swims across. I hear a low howl, then a higher howl. And then I hear some sounds I don't know words for—something growly but not a growl, something like a moan but not, something slightly like a bark. I think it's nearby, but I don't see anything. Is it a wolf? I doubt it—it sounds too odd, too varied, it goes on so long, and besides, it's just too much to hope for. Man? Man and dog? It must be a big dog, I decide.

But Mary Lea, who has stayed lower in the valley while I climbed a hill, can see it, and it *is* a wolf, a black one. More, she sees the puff of white steam from its upturned head an instant before she hears each sound. Later she'll tell me that this is one of those near-religious moments of her life, the kind of moment that is so beautiful and so incredible that it takes your breath—this sight she'd never hoped to see, will probably never see again, this evidence of exuberant survival in the face of all the damage we've done to the world.

Finally the six valley wolves file back across the road and climb to a small shelf on the hill, where they meet the howler in a welcoming flurry of dust and waving tails.

~

By definition, I have thought, true miracles are not created by humans. We can't bring back life once it has vanished; in the face of extinction, we're helpless. When the apostle John told of Jesus raising Lazarus after four days in the grave, his was not a story of the actions of a man (though it is here—in the Bible's shortest verse—that, faced by loss, "Jesus wept") but a story of the signs and wonders that convinced a people they were seeing the son of God.

Sometimes I think human life is a tug-of-war between two kinds of people: those who mostly destroy and those who mostly try to protect, restore, or create. And I often feel that the destroyers usually win, even if they are fewer in number, simply because it's so much easier and quicker to break than to make something. So I suppose that maybe when the creators triumph over the destroyers, when we mend something we have shattered, a kind of miracle occurs. Is our restoration of wolves to Yellowstone a miracle? It feels like one to me, or at least like grace: what once we lost, we now have found.

~

August 2004. Sometimes I come alone to this quiet old cabin in the Uncompaghre Mountains of Colorado to think and write. I'm here now to think about looking for wolves.

I take my grilled cheese and tomato sandwich out to the back porch of the cabin and sit on a ratty lawn chair. Hummingbirds zoom around a feeder, ravens dot the meadow, a chipmunk edges closer.

I think about how in all my wolf-searching, despite the association of wolves with unpeopled wilderness, I've never been alone. I think about the path I've traced, from northern Minnesota to the Arctic coast to Alaska to Wyoming, circling away and then closer to my Colorado home, and about how the wolves have been moving south toward Colorado at the same time. I think about the Yellowstone wolf that was killed by a car in the center of this state just a couple of months ago, and about the possibility that wolves may soon return to the mountains just south of me.

And I think about how, for me, wolves began in the realms of history, myth, and dream, of imagination, desire, and apparition. How they've emerged now into actuality, inhabited real bodies, here and now, heart-

and-lung, bone-and-muscle wolves doing regular wolfish things, swimming across rivers, wagging their tails, making noise. How their return has begun to move beyond miracle into plain reality, and how this may after all be the greater wonder.

On the path just to my west, between meadow and aspen grove, a coyote trots casually by, then speeds up to a slow lope when he notices me.

For the first time in my life, I'm watching a coyote in Colorado knowing that a few years from now, sitting right here in the same lawn chair, I might see a wolf.

Susan J. Tweit

Susan J. Tweit is the author of eight books on nature in the American West and often writes from her home in Salida, Colorado, for "Writers on the Range," the Denver Post, *and the* Mountain Mail. *Focusing on the wolf to whom we have dedicated this book, the female who traveled alone from Yellowstone to central Colorado, she surveys the topic of wolf recovery and thinks about how these wild animals "make the place whole."*

Wolf 293

One foggy September morning I slipped out of a motel room at dawn with my Great Dane, Isis, headed for the banks of the Yellowstone River in Gardener, Montana, just north of Yellowstone National Park. Clouds hung low over the peaks. As we trotted along, I sucked in breaths of air that smelled like snow.

Isis suddenly stopped in the middle of the street. Her dish-antenna-sized ears swung forward and her ruff stood erect. An instant later, I caught the sound she'd heard: a couple of distant barks followed by a long ululating howl. That drawn-out howl came again, full-throated notes starting low, rising to a peak, then slowly sinking away: "Ooooooooooooooooooo!"

"Wolves!" I said to Isis and raced back to the motel to rouse my husband.

Later that day, peering through a telescope as wet flakes of snow fell around us, we watched a pack relaxing: five wolves, two black, one Husky-gray, and two coyote-colored, curled up and snoozing in the autumn-dry grass. One stood up, shook the snow off its thick fur, stretched languidly—I could almost hear its spine cracking—and then curled up again, very much at home.

Driving back to Colorado, I played that image and the dawn howls over in my mind. I'd read the research on wolves' return to Yellowstone. Their contribution to the health of the ecosystems was clear from the data: the elk were wary again, moving like wild herds rather than zoo animals, and their bloated populations were shrinking; willow, aspen, and cottonwood stands were beginning a patchy recovery after decades of unchecked elk browsing; coyote numbers had dropped, grizzly bears were again dining at wolf kills, and beaver, long absent, had returned to the northern part of the park. Essential ecological relationships, broken by wolves' absence, were mending.

But it wasn't until I heard and saw wolves reinhabiting that landscape that I grasped the deeper truth at the heart of their return: wolves make the place whole. Without them, it was a tamer landscape, less challenging and also less inspiring, a shadow of its full self.

Will we be able to welcome wolves home to the rest of the West the way we've embraced them in Yellowstone, where park officials say they are the most popular wildlife in a landscape crammed with charismatic species?

It's not clear. But gray wolves are not waiting for our invitation; they are already dispersing throughout the West. In June 2004, a young female wolf made it as far as central Colorado: her body—belly full of deer meat, legs broken—was found on the shoulder of Interstate 70 west of Idaho Springs. Her radio collar identified her as Wolf 293, a member of the Swan Lake Pack from northern Yellowstone, some five hundred miles away.

What was she doing so far from home? Searching for the stuff of myth and literature: love and fortune.

Wolf 293 was just a pup in January 2003 when biologists shot her with a tranquilizer dart and attached a radio collar to track her movements. She spent her first year learning wolf ways with her siblings in her natal pack, one of Yellowstone's oldest and most successful wolf packs. She was a year old—almost mature—when she was last located by radio telemetry near Mammoth Hot Springs in January 2004. After that, Wolf 293 vanished from researchers' contact until she was found dead in Colorado six months later.

Apparently, Wolf 293's pack had no room for another potentially dominant adult female, so in her second spring, she struck out to find her own space—a territory and a mate. Her quest was not so different from that of our young, who leave home and often wander widely before settling into a career and family. What makes Wolf 293's journey extraordinary is that she trekked hundreds of miles, alone, on her quest.

Before Wolf 293, the last known wild gray wolf in this part of Colorado was killed in the Conejos Valley in 1945, the victim of a culture that fervently believed that predators like wolves, mountain lions, and grizzly bears were evil, symbols of a wild that needed to be tamed to make the world safe.

Wolves certainly seem to fit the part. They haunt our species' earliest myths and dreams, their eyeshine glittering in the darkness, their shaggy forms patiently circling us with evil intent—fangs ready. The very word "wolf" conjures up the terror of the wild unknown, as with werewolves, those half-human, half-beast creatures whose bodies turn lupine (Latin for "wolflike") and bloodthirsty with each full moon. Or Lupus, the mysterious and often fatal chronic illness named for the facial rash it causes, thought to resemble the bite of a wolf.

We fear wolves, sure that they lust for our flesh, even though the record to the contrary is extensive: for at least the past century, no cases of healthy, wild wolves killing humans can be documented in North America. We are rarely the easiest or most available prey.

Once we befriended these enemies. Some fourteen thousand years ago, we began domesticating wolves in a tacit bargain: space at the campfire and scraps in return for companionship and devotion. The result: domestic dogs all descended from wolves. Nowadays we dote on these pet canids, from tiny terriers to Great Danes like Isis. Unfortunately, our companions are not as discriminating as their ancestors: our pets kill an average of thirteen people each year. What does it say about us that we harbor pit bulls, the breed most likely to kill humans, but we cannot tolerate wolves?

We cringe when we see wolves circling a cow elk and leaping to tear chunks of flesh out of her flanks. What we read as savagery is, in fact, adherence to the code of genetic survival: an understanding that death feeds continuing life. We insulate ourselves from our part in killing by buying our food neatly packaged and processed. But when faced with starvation, we lose our squeamishness, leaping for flesh just as quickly as any hungry wolf.

Wolves kill to settle conflicts as well, but they cannot touch our species' record: We killed an estimated ten million of our fellow humans in World War I alone, and fifty million in World War II. Although we flinch at killing to eat, we seem to have accepted killing each other as a reasonable way to "even the score," whether in the fantasy world of movies, television, and video games, or in the reality of schools and neighborhood streets.

Perhaps the sin of wolves is their lack of deference to our self-defined rank as top of the heap. From their point of view, humans constitute either prey or competition—no more, no less. They don't care what we think. We have grown increasingly less tolerant of those who look, act, or see the world differently than we do. The more insular we become, taking refuge inside gated communities, fearful of faces shadowed by turban, tattoo, or chador, unable to respect diversity, whether in dress, speech, culture, language, or worldview, the more we need wildness like wolves to restore our balance.

Wildness reminds us that life is not simple, truth is not black and white; that sameness is slow death and diversity rejuvenating. Look at Yellowstone: without wolves, elk herds exploded, eating themselves out of house and home, destroying habitat for other species, and setting the stage for devastating epidemics like Chronic Wasting Disease. Only a decade after the wolves' return, biologists cautiously conclude that wolves have opened up niches for dozens of other species, leading to a landscape healthier for all.

Wolves are native to western landscapes: these wild canids were here long before our own species reached this continent. Until I heard and saw Yellowstone's wolves, though, I didn't realize how much their absence diminishes the rest of the West. Without wolves, an essential kind of wildness is missing from this spare mix of peak and valley, canyon and mesa.

We cannot precisely trace Wolf 293's route from Yellowstone to Colorado. I imagine her trotting steadily south along the flanks of the mountains, edging around open basins, and stopping each evening on some ridge or hill to broadcast her yearning call. She stands, tips her muzzle to the sky, and hurls that rich, full-throated wolf howl across the landscape: "Ooooooooooooooooooooooo!"

Then she listens, ears pricked forward, swiveling to catch any response. But there is no answering call. She tips her muzzle up again and sends forth another howl. She listens. Still nothing. She trots on. Each night, she curls up, nose under tail, and drifts off to sleep. Just before dawn, she stretches, sniffs the wind for news, and tries again: still, no answer.

She trots on, hunting, resting—fulfilling her immediate needs, but driven to search for more: home, family. Finally, continuing her journey south, she is hit crossing the river of traffic on Interstate 70. She drags herself off the roadway, and dies, alone.

When I learned of Wolf 293 and her solitary quest, I wanted to howl my own anguish into the night sky. My grief was as much for myself, and my home landscape, as for her. "I knew the song the wolf sang," writes Kathleen Dean Moore. "The first two tones make an augmented fourth, a dissonant interval, like the first two notes of 'Maria' in West Side Story. It's an interval of yearning, of hope—the sound of human longing."

I long for the day when we embrace the return of wildness, without fear and prejudice. When instead of rejecting or ignoring those who see the world differently, we seek to learn from them. When those who are fundamentally different, yet alike in spirit are respected. When no one—human or other animal—is lonely for the sound of a kindred voice. When we welcome wolves as fellow westerners whose quest for life is so much like ours.

On our daily dawn walk, Isis and I stop in the open landscape beyond town, ears perked, listening intently for news of the wild. I hope for the howl of wolves, home again in our part of the West.

Maria Melendez

Maria Melendez has lived in Colorado, worked at the Teton Science School, and taught creative writing and multiethnic literature and environment courses as writer-in-residence at the University of California–Davis Arboretum and as a faculty member at Saint Mary's College in Indiana. Her first full-length book of poetry is forthcoming from the University of Arizona Press. "Aullido" ("Howl") calls the wolf back to its old homes in the Southern Rockies—places from which its spirit has never vanished.

Aullido

In the Sierra Madre
they say, *"El alma de*
un lobo nunca desaparecía
de este mundo"—

a wolf's spirit never disappears
        from the forest.
"Siempre su espíritu
        estaba pendiente de vigilar

todo lo que había
        a su alrededor;
era el protector
        de los bosques."

Can you picture a wolf's spirit?
        It's not the gray, wispy thing
screen-printed as background
        on countless tees.

It's solid as granite,
          forged in fire, firm
as the basement rock
          of the Rocky Mountains.

Can you picture a wolf's spirit
          as protector, or as sculptor,
of the pines, the spruce, the firs,
          even the elk?

Too, it is mammalian and familial:
          there is a *loba* spirit flowing
in your breast milk and in that
          of elk, moose, and deer.

So come back here, loba,
          recuerda estas montañas,
mother mountains:

San Juan Range, Sierra del Huacha, Culebra Range, Spanish Peaks, Front
Range, Snowy Range, Sierra de la Encantada, Sawatch Range, Gore
Range, White Mountains, Black Range, Mogollon Mountains, Burro
Mountains, Sierra del Nido, Sierra Madre Occidental.

Living wolf, spirit in flesh,
breathe here,
walk here, recall these places
you never left.

Glance again in time's long mirror
and recognize yourself.

A Howling from the Belly

It's no secret that the return of wolves is a prospect that raises strong passions of many kinds. For many, the wolf's quintessentially wild howl signals everything that wildness suggests: our ancient primal and cultural fears of powerful predators and, indeed, of all threats to our safety; the tensions between environmentalists and ranchers about the ecological value of wolves and their danger to livestock (still the chief impediment to wolf recovery efforts); our new fears of living in a society that has lost its authentic contact with nature; our deep yearning for a restored world. Just as these passions saturate the debates about wolf restoration, so also do they drive the poems and essays in this section.

Clifford Pfeil

Clifford Pfeil, who lives in Tucson, Arizona, is the author of the children's book Benjamin the Meetinghouse Mouse *and a teacher of English to refugees from politics and war. He is also a retired music composition teacher, and his poem builds on his knowledge of music to describe and imagine the wolf's howl—a sound that haunts many of the following pieces.*

Wolf Tone

The wolf tone breaks
the logic of the instrument,
affects a certain pitch,
shudders up its backbone,
as the framework of a troika
shudders over ice,
and a storm of forest wolves
closing at the flank.
It's a howling from the belly
of the instrument, a cello maybe,
playing Bach before the guests,
and vodka on the table.
It's an error in the making
of the instrument, the maplewood
uneven, the f holes shocked,
the post a fraction out of place.

Not in the least an error for the wolves,
running in their forest home,
calling their compatriots,
diving past the splayed design of trees,
at ease with blowing branches,
entrained like flying leaves
into the rhythms of the land.

Susan Zwinger

Susan Zwinger's most recent book about nature and the environment is The Hanford Reach. *Though she spent many of her formative years in Colorado Springs, she now lives on an island in Puget Sound and is currently teaching for the North Cascades Institute, the Heritage Institute, and The Nature Conservancy in Oregon. For her, the "soul-carving" howl of the wolf is the sign of "pure wilderness."*

Why Wild Wolves

My formative years were sculpted in the wilds of Colorado, but it was not until many years later that I heard the sound of true wilderness. As a teen, I camped and climbed fourteeners with the Girl Scouts. As college students, we took furtive trips out West to backpack every chance we could. In my twenties, men friends trained me on hair-raising rock climbs and taught me ice-ax arrests. Growing up in Colorado Springs, I had molten Pikes Peak granite in my arteries and considered myself a child of the wilderness.

Yet it was not until a five-month solo road trip through Alaska in 1988 that I first heard pure wilderness and experienced how Colorado must have been 150 years ago—wild and wooly, miners' gouges helter-skelter, jagged peaks full of snowfields and glaciers. Streams so thick with fish you could dip-net them. Forests full of mink, bear, wolverine—and wolves. Mostly unencumbered by roads, and those roads made up of appalling mud.

I gave myself the life-changing challenge of traveling through Alaska, including up the Haul Road toward Prudhoe Bay, in a small black pickup named Die Fledermazda. During the long daylight hours, I wore myself out by exploring, gathering, identifying, climbing, driving, and keeping up an illustrated field journal seventeen hours a day. Even though I was theoretically grieving the end of a relationship, I had never been so ecstatic. Animals so new to me as to be shocking, up and walked into my camp—

moose and wolverine. I could crouch by a lake of dying sockeye for hours watching this beautiful red and chartreuse fish expire and be dragged up on shore by eagles and bears to feed the great trees. This was truly a healthy ecosystem, a phenomenon I had never experienced—not even high in the Rockies.

One night, north of Valdez, surrounded by immense, flowing glaciers, I fell to sleep in a whiteout. Through the fog of sleep a sound hollowed out my bones and pulled up the waking consciousness of my prehistoric hunting ancestors through spirals of DNA. My adrenaline was on full throttle. What had I heard?

I was already tense. Two weeks earlier an earthquake had violently shaken the ground beneath me on Lake Eklutna fifty miles north of Anchorage, and now I was afraid of tidal waves or steeply stacked talus cliffs above. It dawned on me that up here in the North, wilderness could kill! Now, nerves on alert, I grabbed my coat, slid on untied mountain boots, and sprang from under the truck canopy.

Again, through a whiteout with mist as thick as slurping, freezing ocean, sound waves warbled toward me from very close by. Something otherworldly. One after another after another, the voices piled in layers of sound.

Wolves howl purposefully and artfully on adjacent or harmonic notes until the complex sound waves multiply and multiply exponentially— eight wolves sound like seventeen. The individuals seemed aware of one another's tones and created an orchestral blend. Here was intelligent communication before the night's hunt. My hearing was magnified by the lack of sight. That sound was so eerie, so soul-carving, that I slept fitfully all night long waiting for a new chorus before dawn. Sure enough, bursting with news of the hunt, the wolves greeted each other at 4:00 A.M. They began low-pitched, as if through the earth, and rose in a quavering crescendo. This time the howls were more varied, as if containing specific information. Yet again the wolves vibrated my bone marrow and carved out my soul. This sound cannot be captured in words any more than sex can be described to a virgin.

Now, I live on an island in Washington and often seek wilderness through its rugged, young mountain ranges, or up into British Columbia and the Yukon. Wherever I travel, I keep seeking this sound. I howl for wolves in the North Cascades of Washington and the interior of British Columbia where they supposedly live. Nada. I am forever in search of that intimate howl of pure wilderness that awakens the wildest and most authentic me.

Laura Paskus

Laura Paskus, a former archaeologist, lives in Paonia, Colorado, and is the assistant editor at High Country News. *Her essay imagines the wolf's howl as a spur to both primal fear and hope, a respite from and possible remedy for the world of distressing politics and environmental damage.*

The Wolf at the Door

There is an expression for my condition: The wolf is at the door. But I want the wolf at the door. I am tired of living in a world without wolves. —Charles Bowden

On September 10, 2004, three friends and I drove across western Colorado and on into Utah. We arrived in the desert hours after dark and camped not too far off the interstate. Even though everyone was exhausted, we lit a fire—a blissful reward for having made it through another George W. Bush–era workweek. Of the four of us, three are environmental journalists, and the other runs a small nonprofit dedicated to river restoration. We regularly suffer defeat and disappointment.

In the last few years, I've watched my government commit countless acts of terrorism against this nation's environment. From increased oil and gas drilling, to the weakening of the National Environmental Policy Act and pollution laws, to the suppression of federal scientists, the White House and Congress have waged what some call an unprecedented assault on the environment. And they've done this while claiming to protect us from other threats.

For the four of us, any weekend that doesn't require work calls for getting out of range of the news. As one friend wrapped himself in his sleeping bag near the fire and marveled at the stars shooting across the sky above—five, he counted out to us—he sighed, "Life is *bueno.*" He paused, "Well, it's not really, but. . . ."

But out here life is *bueno.* Even if the world is falling apart, you can't do anything about it. All you can do out here is fall asleep, hope a scorpion won't find its way inside your bag, say a prayer of thanks for the Milky Way. And if a coyote or a wolf jars you awake at night, all you can do is hope you'll have the presence of mind to remember the sound in the morning.

Fear will always define that moment when wolves and humans interact—whether they meet face-to-face, snout to lips; or whether the weary backpacker hears the distant howl in the middle of the night. I'm not talking about the fear that reintroduced wolves will lead to lost revenue and tattered cattle; nor am I speaking of the irrational wolf-eats-child scenario.

I'm referring to what happens to your heart and brain and gut in the middle of the night when you hear the howl of some red-blooded canine. Whether you consider wolves foes or friends, the jolt of primal fear is the same. Something is out there, and you are vulnerable. Decisions must be made, resources and skills evaluated. An activist friend who was emerging from the Gila Wilderness a few years ago told me what he felt when he heard the sound of wolves howling in the night: In that first instant, he explained, his heart was held tight in a grip of pure fear. But a moment after the sound woke him, he rejoiced—rejoiced that they were real, that they were surviving.

Being startled awake by the howling of a wolf would do wonders for my soul. Perhaps a jolt of primal fear could knock about the other fears rattling around in my head. And perhaps, a moment or two after awakening, I could feel the hope that so often eludes me lately. For truly, that howl represents hope—hope not only that wolves will survive, but that there are people out there who care enough to ensure they do.

Two mornings later, I'm sleeping at the foot of a sandstone cliff that leans sixty or seventy feet above my bag. When I wake before dawn to sand dusting my face from above—crows taking flight, perhaps—I'm startled, but not alarmed. I listen to my friends sleeping nearby, feel my dog pressed against my legs (he's doing his best to edge me off the ThermaRest), look up at the few lingering stars in the predawn sky, and I know I can snatch an hour more of sleep here on the sand. There's no sense in giving in to irrational fears. I won't wake everyone up by traipsing around our camp and moving my sleeping bag. I refuse to set a new print in the sand. Were I trapped within my four walls at home, I'd have been up hours ago.

The noises that wake me at home aren't terror-inducing by any means—no fanged creatures, no looming disasters, no sand falling from a crumbly sandstone cliff above my head. Instead, I am awakened at night by things I read and write about all day: coalbed methane drilling in the valley where I live, and in fact, all across the West; congressional budgets for new nuclear weapons and plans to ship waste from state to state, country to country. Scientists say there are pharmaceuticals in the drinking water, endocrine disrupters in the fat of arctic polar bears and genetically modified organisms in our food. There's also the dry bed of my beloved Rio Grande, drill rigs pressed up against wilderness areas and endless expanses of paved-over, franchise-filled suburbs. At home, I wake and I fret. And sadly, there's no escape from these things at dawn. Each morning, the cycle starts again: I am a journalist, and it's my job to make other people aware of the things I worry about all night.

But this morning in the desert, I fail to worry. Instead, I hunker back into the sand, look up the scale of the cliff, and feel grateful for the breath all around me: the snores of my friends, the quiet breath of the desert at dawn, the lack of tightness in my chest.

~

Returning home from the desert on Sunday, I avoid showering all night because I want to smell like dirt and sweat and all the things I believe are good and pure. Eventually, I take a bath; I want to see the sand pooled around the drain.

Being away from my world for just the weekend, I'm reminded that primal fear makes sense. A wolf waking someone from a sound slumber makes sense. Whether you hate wolves or love them, any one of us would wake with a start, a pounding heart. What you do next is up to you. Once you're awake, you can choose to reach for a gun or lie back and smile, reassured that reintroducing predators is the right thing to do in today's world of obscene human privilege, resource wars, and national security hype.

The time has come: we need more wolves. A world without wolves is less than a world. A world without fear is also a world without love, without passion, without righteous goodness. A world without wolves is not the world in which we should want to live. It is time for the wolf to be at the door again.

Michael Annis

Michael Annis is senior editor and designer for all Howling Dog Press publications and recordings and the author of poetry and speculative non-fiction anthologized most recently in the Silo Inspection Reports: Adopt-a-Silo Action. *He lives in Berthoud, Colorado. "Portage" reenacts in vivid detail the awe and fear he feels on meeting a wolf deep in Ontario's wilderness.*

Portage

—for John Frankenberg

Our eighth day of solitude, deep in the raw Ontario wilderness
(freed from the suffocating grip of cities and humans for three)
where dry-rot signs warned "NO," scrawled an uncertain way;

a billion stars in the canopy, half of them streaking in flight
across the shimmering rim of the nascent Northern Lights
in September's deep night chill; surviving on bluegill, bass,

walleye, rosehips, jerky, grouse, berries, coffee, trail mix;
canoeing across lakes called Smallmouth, Sturgeon, LaCroix,
Sark, Kawnipi, Pickerel—now this far up, mostly nameless

as this portage in daybreak drizzle fog, a single narrow pass
a hundred ten miles out of range of doctors, phone, radio, mail.
Breaking camp, you fell behind; slung canoe on my shoulders,

sleeping bags, backpack across chest, I lumbered the trail,
climbing over treefall, through thickets, around boulders,
my eyes down, scanning ahead, scrutinizing wet ground

and tracks of moose, huge as paddles, where settled night rains
in small clear pools teeming fresh reflections of trees and sky,
I rounded a bend, stopping dead still in glowing yellow eyes

from the gray-black face of a timber wolf who made no sound
lapping rainwater from moose tracks, front legs splayed, tail
tucked under, ears back, muscles along neck, sides, and thighs

rippling with each drink, hindquarters ready, as close to me as the rise
of my shadow, as near as one leap, an intruder in his threatened domain
gazed steadily staring full face, gray winter coat tufting patches of snow.

Frozen captive in his primeval beauty—not with terror, *awe*—
    I knew how
he could tear out my throat before I dropped the canoe,
    emitted one lone cry;
knew he could sense panic—could *smell fear*—as my courage waned.

Yet he, the wiser, whose feral jaws could snuff my soul, allowed his bane
pale passage, his burden of freedom bestowed mercy,
    enveloped my epiphany.
Fluffing his tail, he trotted away, curled back his lips, smiling into my fear.

While you, soon coming up behind me, were baffled,
    muttering in disbelief,
"Mike—*this is crazy*—look at these tracks. There's been a huge
    dog up here."
Still shuddering, I whispered, "No, wolf! *Timber wolf*—
    should've killed me."

David Schelly

David Schelly is a student at Colorado State University focusing on environmental affairs and communication. During an encounter with wolves in the wilds of British Columbia, he remembers his ancestors' battle against wolves on their ranch in eastern Colorado and thinks about the fear these predators evoke—and likely feel.

The South Platte Wolf

A woman from the forestry company drives me as far down the road as she can without getting stuck in the mud, as far north into the interior of British Columbia as I can get without paddling or walking. Her name is Claudette. She's a rough woman with a deep voice and the smell of stale cigarettes. "You're braver than Daniel Boone," she says, but I feel more foolish than brave.

Last night, Claudette's friend on the west side of the Coastal Mountains took me to a fiftieth wedding anniversary. The festivities were dampened for me when the locals told me I was going to die. They told me stories of car-sized grizzlies stalking unsuspecting hikers and said the bears were trying to fatten up for winter this time of year. The interior bears struggle to find their food, they explained, since the spawning steelhead can't make it past the waterfalls in the mountains. I'm trying to believe that a gun or bear spray is unnecessary—they would give me a false confidence that could provoke a charge—but the locals did not agree. When I told them I was going unarmed, they looked at me as if I were crazy.

Claudette drops me off in a light rain. According to my map, the river is to the southwest, so I drag my boat and gear down a worn road through puddles and mud. I walk through a forest of thick lodgepole pines that are skinny and tall from cold temperatures and a dry climate. I wonder if my homemade blanket will be sufficient. There's not much underbrush, but the trees are so dense I can't see far and not much light gets through the canopy. The forest is dark and quiet. Even the birds seem to be scared. The infrequency of their single chirps makes me wonder if they're alerting each other of danger.

This is the first day of a solo kayaking expedition northwest through the interior plateau of the Chilcotin region, over the Coastal Mountains and around the coast to the town of Bella Coola. It is also my first time alone in grizzly country and the first time I've felt like prey.

I wonder where my fear comes from. The only large predators in my homeland of Colorado were bobcats, mountain lions, and coyotes. I saw a bobcat once, in a flash behind a bush, and I saw a lion from a distance, across a river, sprinting through an opening. I remember that when I was a child, my family heard nighttime noises in the backyard and in the morning found the remains of a half-eaten deer carcass with a broken neck. I knew not to go running behind the house during dusk or dawn when the lions were hunting, but I was not afraid—I always thought I could fight a lion off if I saw the attack coming. Coyotes would howl like dog pups every night behind our house. They kept their dens in caves near the top of a mountain where I found their scat, along with balls of gray fur and pieces of rabbit bone. At night they ran through the valley snatching nesting chickens and geese, but they were harmless to humans.

My fear was not learned but seems to have been in my blood from birth—as a bird, still blind and flightless in the nest, seems to be afraid of a human hand.

I walk the muddy road to the river, paddle all day, and make my first camp, grilling fish for supper. I keep the fire going until an hour after dark and then climb into my bivy sack. Listening to the stillness of the frozen September air, I feel utterly alone.

Suddenly I hear a howling across the river, a new sound to me. It's not a coyote. This sound is a deep howl, like a huge hound calling a mate. It has to be a wolf. Zipped shut in my bivy, I feel as if the wolf and I are the only things in existence—the slight breeze and flowing water are muted to the background of the howling and my own thoughts. My heartbeat is in my ears and my breath is pressing loudly against my bivy sack. Every movement I make shuffles the nylon fabric from my blanket and interrupts the silence around me. The fear in my blood is telling me to climb out of the bivy and find my knife, but I don't want to move in case the wolf hears me. It must know I'm here.

Not since my grandfather's time were there wolves where I grew up on the plains of Colorado. There a single wolf used to howl across the South Platte River. This was back when Aldo Leopold was anxious to see every last wolf and lion exterminated, when he wanted to save the deer and my family wanted to save their cattle and their livelihood. The South Platte wolf threatened my family's existence, so they sent dogs after it.

More than one wolf now echoes across the river. It sounds like they are barking and yelping and playfully fighting, over an elk, perhaps, or a deer or moose. Or just chasing each other through a meadow and nipping at heels under the light of the half-moon. I'm guessing it's a small pack, no more than five.

Time passes slowly, and the wolves' cries ring in my head. Even when the night is quiet again, sleep will not come.

I wonder what the wolves are doing so close to me, in the interior where they could live many lives without seeing a person. During all the talk about predators last night, the local people made no mention of wolves. Wolves are different from grizzlies. Bears flock to town dumps and eat barking dogs; they wander to the smell of civilization where armed mushroom hunters startle them and make them afraid. Wolves are more cautious. They stay away from humans, maybe because they have fear in their blood, too.

That wolf on the Colorado plains by my family's homestead had a tough time. Not only did ranchers chase wolves with killer dogs, but they also set traps, left poison, and shot at any wolf they saw. Four generations before me, a man in my family killed what he believed to be the last buffalo on the plains. For previous generations of wolves, buffalo were a main food source. By the time my grandfather was born, the plains wolves had no buffalo to hunt. Their easiest prey were cattle overgrazing the prairie.

Perhaps the wolves across the river have a memory of cattle and ranchers and hound dogs.

I wake up with the sun and remain zipped shut for a while, allowing the light frost to melt from the forest floor before I get up to strip naked and put on my wet gear and pack my boat. Today, the sounds from the night seem like a dream, ghost sounds from my family's past. They seem no different from the dream I actually had, of a grizzly sniffing at my head. I woke up trembling, imagining the wind was the breathing of a bear deciding if I was food. Dreams are difficult to separate from reality out here.

I paddle my kayak through shallow, slow-moving water where the river is wide. Much of the time my boat scrapes over unavoidable rocks, many of them big enough to stop my movement altogether. At times I have to get out of my boat and pull it behind me, slogging my way through ankle-deep water until the river looks deep enough to float. Other times I shuffle my way from one rock to the next by reaching both arms into the water and pulling and pushing my weight forward.

I paddle around a large bend in the river and no longer know my direction. The river has been shallow for a while, but not so much that I am going to get out of my boat. I paddle until I am stuck on a rock, half the size of my boat and just below the surface.

About a hundred yards ahead, three animals come out from a stand of willows onto a large sandbar. At first their long, slender legs and large, muscular bodies remind me of horses, but they are wolves—two of them black and the third gray.

They don't even glance in my direction. I watch them for a while and wonder what to do, and then they trot in single file through the knee-deep water to the other bank and run in my direction. They run to the bank closest to me and then turn in to the bushes.

I know of no documented wolf attack on a human, but I doubt they have ever seen a kayak before; maybe they don't know that they don't eat small plastic boats. I don't have a lot of protection: I have a helmet on and multiple layers of clothing, along with my life jacket that is filled with a thin layer of steel for protection against rocks. I have a river knife and a paddle with blades that might do some damage to a wolf. But all I really have is a theory that they will not generally attack people.

They come out of the bushes, still ignoring me, and run downstream. They cross the river and stop on the sandbar where they hesitate before entering the willows. I reach my paddle into the water and shimmy myself off the rock and float slowly in their direction, up to and past their sandbar.

I look back and see a black wolf peering at me, its head half-hidden by a clump of willows. It is looking me in the eyes and its head is lowered—in the same way a submissive dog's would be if it knew it was in trouble—and its ears are slightly back. The wolf's dark eyes gaze at me with curious hesitation, as if I am a threat.

Our eye contact lasts one long breath. Then the wolf pulls back behind the willows and is gone.

I round the next corner. All that remains of wolves are the dreamy sounds from the night and a hazy image behind a stand of willows. My fear is the same fear experienced by generations of ancestors who lived among wolves that threatened their cattle. The wolf could have the same memory in his blood: he, too, may know what it feels like to be prey.

Mary Crow

Mary Crow is Colorado's poet laureate and the recipient of numerous prizes and fellowships. Her newest book is The High Cost of Living. *In this retelling of an Eastern European story made famous in Willa Cather's novel* My Ántonia, *she immerses us in our culture's tradition of imagining wolves as ravening beasts. But this poem also reminds us that literature has the power to make—and remake—lingering images and attitudes.*

Canis lupus, Family Canidae

I
The gray wolf is a god of the dead,
spirit caught in the last sheaf—
Oats-wolf, Rye-wolf, Barley-wolf—
sometimes the scythe can kill him.
After the threshing: the wolf-puppet
paraded from farm to farm.

II
Shadows dodge among trees
as the sledges return from the wedding,
a howling gathering on the hills
as dozens, then hundreds swell into a black swarm,
spooking the horses
till they slip on ice, tipping the last sledge:
howls blot out
the screams of horses and guests.
Panic spreads to the lead
sledge with the wedding couple as the black
wave seeps its black ink
onward and the driver whispers,

Throw her over! Throw her over!
The horrified groom holds onto his bride as the driver
tries to wrench her
free and the howls sweep closer and closer,
the horses snort.
The bride falls, the driver whips his horses,
the wolves leap, and the sledge escapes.

III
Gray wolf, he's taking the bride
on his plunderings, into the sheaves
of wheat, into the final threshing.

John Calderazzo

John Calderazzo contemplates the fear of wolves in the context of other cultural fears—of killer bees, mega-volcanoes, terrorists, and other versions of apocalypse. He teaches creative nonfiction writing at Colorado State University. His newest book is Rising Fire: Volcanoes and Our Inner Lives.

Apocalypse Dogs

"Put *wolves* back in Colorado?" said my Bellvue neighbor, Mack, as though there were something wrong with our phone connection, or with me. "Aw, you don't want to know what I think about wolves."

But I did—I had been asking friends, neighbors, and even local store-keepers about this issue, and all had either liked the idea or said they didn't know enough about it to form an opinion. Until Mack. Now, as he dropped into silence, I pictured him tugging at one end of his droopy moustache, deciding whether to say more.

I had known him over the years to be witty and self-deprecating: a knowledgeable and thoughtful guy. He grew up in the farmland of eastern Colorado, wrangled horses in mountain towns during his twenties, and now makes his living jetting around the country singing cowboy songs that are witty and self-deprecating, too. I thought of him as a campfire troubadour, an Old West/New West man. This meant that while he kept a horse and a pickup with a gun rack, he also packed a laptop full of constantly evolving jokes and sometimes goofy song lyrics.

Finally he said, "Well, I hate wolves! I hate the bastards because they love to kill. They'll tear open the throats of a whole herd of sheep just for fun. They'll run down an elk and hamstring it for the hell of it. Every outfitter I know hates the bastards, too. How's that for an answer?"

Over the next few days, I thought a great deal about Mack's tirade, so charged with sudden anger and soaked in Old Testament dread. Where had all that come from?

Apparently, about seventy percent of Coloradoans say they support the reintroduction of wolves to some of their old habitats. But I've begun to notice that inside the opposing thirty percent, who often sound reasonable enough to me, lurk some doomsayers who can make Mack look like an optimist. These are the folks who predict the ravaging of what seems like every cow west of the 100th meridian—plus, if you're not careful, maybe your little dog, too.

This despite the opinions of practically every wildlife biologist I've read about or spoken to at CSU, where I teach. They argue that *Canis lupus* rarely did and rarely will behave in these ways. The scientists are not claiming that these comeback wolves will lie down with lambs in some Bambi World of the future. They are saying that while wolves will hunt in packs and kill some domestic animals, they are as far from the glittery-eyed serial killers of legend as I am from Jack the Ripper.

So why do these mythic exaggerations persist and grow, even among otherwise reasonable people like Mack? This isn't the frontier West where every coyote within shooting range was strung up on a fence as a lesson to the howling wilderness, and where almost nobody questioned the bounties that eventually wiped out all of Colorado's wolves. Wolves: those Apocalypse dogs that supposedly circled the campfire, snarling and waiting for the coals to die, just as they had waited in the dark forests of Europe where most of these myths were born. In the nineteenth and early twentieth centuries, when the Colorado guns were blazing, nobody had heard of an "ecosystem" with its interdependent parts. But they knew Satan, and his face looked a lot like the wolf's. The last wild wolf in our state was shot in 1945.

Now the working group that is pondering their return is also thinking about letting wolves from Yellowstone National Park roam across our border at will. But this time around, it's possible that if you kill one—unless it's in self-defense (which no one in North America has had to do in several hundred years) or in protection of your property—you could pay a hefty fine. Maybe it's the fine that's agitating the doom-and-gloom folks. You know: it's the *government* snarling out there!

Certainly, something odd and edgy is in the air, something larger, I suspect, than an issue of animal reintroduction. It's as though, in some fevered imaginations, wolves have turned into a northern species of killer bees.

Remember them? Stinging hordes imported from Africa to Brazil a few decades ago, they escaped from a box, then crossbred and multiplied in the wild. Year by year they edged north, over the Panama Canal, up through Mexico, up toward Texas and Arizona. They were a terrible threat to the republic, as I recall, invading at about the same time that unprecedented numbers of Mexican, Honduran, and Guatemalan workers were splashing or floating across the Rio Grande. Swarms of them: worker bees, Apocalypse bees.

They've apparently arrived by now. Yet even as they buzz among the bougainvillea of Scottsdale and Sun City, I don't hear much about them anymore. I suppose the dangers that had been exaggerated from afar have fizzled in the up-close light of reality: they are just a bunch of bees.

But recently I've been hearing quite a bit about another of nature's apocalyptic forces: a tremendous volcano bulging up under Yellowstone National Park. According to the more fantastic of these stories, a planet-shaking volcanic eruption may soon blast up through the middle of our first and most famous national park and kill *every living thing within a radius of six hundred miles!* The eruption cloud alone will drop a thick carpet of ash and cinders over most of the continental U.S. This will clog car engines and computers, smother crops, and cause widespread famine, panic, a military takeover of the government, etc. There are web sites devoted to these Nostradamus scenarios.

It is true that a tremendous geothermal engine thrums beneath the park. It feeds the largest collection of geysers anywhere, causes hundreds of tiny earthquakes per year, and has powered some of the most spectacular volcanic eruptions of all time. But the last of those cataclysms broke open the earth more than 600,000 years ago. For decades now, the volcano beneath Yellowstone has been closely monitored, and nothing suggests that this potential weapon of mass destruction will blow in a scary way anytime soon or even, who knows, for another 100,000 years.

The argument for an imminent blast includes the "fact" that another Big One is overdue, a nonsense argument to anyone with the faintest notion of the immensities of geologic time. More ominous "proof" is the discovery a couple of years ago of a bulge in the bottom of Yellowstone Lake. The bulge is indeed there, freshly measured and mapped, but for all geologists know it has sat under the cold water for centuries and centuries, doing nothing.

Yet the Apocalypse dogs howl on. Park rangers have told me that tourists keep asking about the subterranean terrorism. And these are not just the science illiterates talking—the people who actually ask about the On/Off switches to the geysers or the time of year when the deer turn into elk.

I've heard some of the stories myself, in unexpected places. Last year, when I told one of my teaching colleagues that I was about to visit the park, he stopped dead in his tracks and leaned in to me. "Don't you know?" he hissed. "The whole place is about to blow!" At a party a few months later, I heard that millions of us might soon be dead, courtesy of the Yellowstone Big One. The person who told me this has worked for years in a biology lab.

So what's going on here?

Maybe it's that this killer volcano, like the madly ravaging gray wolf, has recently stepped forward to carry on the real work of the African killer bees. That work, I now suspect, is to stand in for some of our culture's largest and most persistent fears. In the early 1990s, in the Southwest, fears grew that too many illegal immigrants were streaming up from the south. In post-9/11 America, we fear that terrorists can cause stunning devastation from anywhere, including inside our own borders.

Terrorists are the ultimate Apocalypse dogs, and they snarl and shape-shift just outside the flickering light of our national consciousness. Moreover, the shadows they throw seem to grow longer by the day: anthrax, Sarin, a plastic bomb in a luggage bin, a poisoned water system, a nuke in a freighter docking in New York Harbor, Boston, San Diego. These are real threats for sure. And I will never forget what a handful of true believers with box cutters did in the skies above my old hometown: the worst ravaging I have ever seen. Terrorists pounce out of nowhere to kill indiscriminately. We have even seen them on videos tearing open the throats of the innocent.

So maybe we *have* returned to the grim old days in which both reasonable and exaggerated fears crouch side by side in the night forests. Maybe our terror of human evil gone wild has morphed into fears of the natural world lurching violently out of control. In response, our guns are once again cocked or blazing. What else besides outright lies or criminal diversions on the part of our government (scare tactics that seem to have worked) can explain why so many otherwise rational people support the disaster in Iraq?

A few weeks after my telephone conversation with Mack, I strolled over to the Wildlife Biology building on the CSU campus. In the first floor hallway of the building stands a large glass case, and in the middle of the case stands an ancient gray wolf. I don't mean that it was old when it was shot, just that it had been on display longer than anyone I talked to could remember—on previous visits I had asked around. It was easy to imagine, now, that it was the last wolf shot in Colorado.

The start of the semester was a still a few days off, so I had the place to myself, which meant that I could sit on the linoleum floor and think in peace. I looked at the glass case and thought about the stories we tell about wolves and other wild animals, and the stories we tell about even wilder and more powerful forces in the world.

Head thrust forward, about thirty inches tall from large paw to shoulder, the wolf stood on sandy, yucca-strewn soil, as though it had climbed a ridge to survey the high plains to the east of campus. It was a majestic pose, I had thought on other visits. The wolf had looked regal and calm, surveying a world, I liked to imagine, of bison herds, free-flowing rivers, and small bands of humans, such as the Arapahoe, who had little knowledge of a bounty or the willful elimination of an entire species.

But now I began to see something new. The wolf's eyes were not quite focused forward. They looked a bit to the side and down, as though it had somehow turned its gaze from the distant horizon to watch the passing feet of what would soon be thousands of people crowding by in the hallway.

These eyes no longer looked regal or calm. They looked worried. They looked wary. They looked like they had just glimpsed a pack of Apocalypse dogs.

Tony Park

Tony Park, chair of Humanities at Aims Community College in Greeley, Colorado, has published poems in Georgia Review, Sonora Review, Southern Review, *and elsewhere. Building on a haunting image from his Wyoming childhood and a dark piece of family history, his poem is a meditation on loss.*

Eyes Already Gone

One fall, when I was ten,
two wooden posts appeared
alongside the road to the ranch,
a quarter mile from Ned's Creek.

One weekend, between them,
a coyote was strung upside down,
its tongue almost touching the ground.

My father said, "That's Lawrence Vest's work,
proof so he gets paid,
a practice that started with wolves,"

as my mother turned to the back seat of the car.
"Your Grandfather Edwin shot one of the last wolves
in Converse County," she said,
"I have a newspaper clipping at home
in the cedar chest." And later
I asked to see it:

*. . . after an exciting bout of a few miscellaneous miles the tired
and frightened wolf sought refuge in a miniature cave beneath*

a cliff of rocks. Edwin shot it as it was hiding there and although
mortally wounded it crept into the aperture. Edwin bravely
followed and there within the darkness of the cave seized the victim
by tail and dragged him to the light. Edwin is a mighty proud boy
and justly so, for we are all proud of him because anyone who rids
the world of one of these pests deserves unlimited credit. . . .

and I can't say I felt in those words
all the bobcats disappearing from the cottonwoods
around the ranch house, or the cottonwoods
dying one by one;
I couldn't see my grandmother's
black cancer growing, or my grandfather,
who spent two years of grieving and dying,
sitting at the kitchen table for hours on end,
his lungs full of fluid, his soul full of whiskey,
he couldn't lie down . . .

but I knew it was wrong
and the world wasn't right.
I looked away each time we drove around the bend
down by Ned's Creek
on the edge of the Pedro Mountains,

that wounded wolf dragged out of its den,
and that coyote crucified upside down,
its tongue hanging out the side of its mouth,
its eyes already gone.

Jana Richman

Jana Richman lives in Salt Lake City, not far from her childhood ranch home. She is the author of Riding in the Shadows of Saints, *in which she recounts a motorcycle journey along the Mormon Trail of her ancestors. Here she looks at the ways in which wolves can bring generations together as much as they have sometimes driven them apart.*

Wild Thoughts

My father and I lean against a four-pole fence separating us from a 2,300-pound black Simmental bull. The bull throws his head and snorts as he strides toward us to reach the manger at our knees where my father has thrown fresh hay. We are all a little wary of one another—the bull of us, us of him, and my father and I of each other.

"He's been a damn good bull," my father says, trying to ease the abiding tension between us. The bull raises his enormous head from the manger to keep an eye on us as he chews methodically. In one smooth movement my father lifts his sweat-stained American Simmental Association ball cap, runs a chapped, arthritic hand over his bald head, and replaces the cap. He then pulls a piece of alfalfa out of the manger and chews on one end. I do the same.

"He looks like a good one," I say, knowing our uneasiness with each other can be pushed aside for moments at a time, but never really expunged. One of us will eventually take a jab at the other. This time I throw the first punch.

"What do you think about the reintroduction of wolves into the Rocky Mountains?" I ask, ready for his answer, prepared for a rant about calves being killed, ranchers' livelihoods being threatened.

"Oh, I don't know," he says slowly. "I guess it always depends on whose ox is being gored, doesn't it?" The bull blows snot from his nose in our direction. I chew harder on my piece of hay, trying to regroup my thoughts after this surprising show of ambivalence from a man who bristles at the mention of any word that could be linked even remotely to an environmental movement. Discussions of "wilderness" and "open space" send his already high blood pressure soaring. The mention of reintroducing a known predator of cattle should have him snorting like the bull.

"If you had asked me that question ten years ago when I was still running cattle up on the Manti-LaSal, I'd probably be more radically opposed to the idea. But I sort of feel like they belong out there. I guess that's not much of an answer to your question, but I just don't know."

I raise my eyes from the cracked leather of my father's cowboy boot propped on the lowest fence pole next to my frayed sandal, and in my peripheral vision I see the profile of his weathered, age-spotted face. Over the last decade—starting about the time he turned seventy—he has sold off about two-thirds of his land and cattle. He never had a large operation to begin with and now keeps only enough to make sure he can still call himself a rancher. About forty head still wearing his "Rafter R" brand graze on about a hundred acres of mostly juniper and rabbitbrush in Rush Valley, Utah, a few miles south of where we now stand at the corrals behind my childhood home.

The bull ducks his head to grab a large mouthful of hay and spews hay leaves into the wind as he pulls his head back up to check our location.

My father and I watch him silently. We are great arguers of the decades-old ranching on public lands versus environmental issues debate—when President Clinton designated the Grand Staircase Escalante National Monument my father and I could barely be in the same room with each other. But every so often we reach an impasse, such as this one regarding wolves, brought about by finding ourselves too close on an issue.

My father breaks the silence. "The problem is there are just too damn many people, and humans have a tendency to think they can manage everything and they really don't manage things very well."

On these two points my father and I are in absolute agreement. And this is where I'm stuck on the wolf reintroduction issue: Wolf Management Plans. The management plans speak of wolves in terms of tourist dollars they might generate weighed against the economic losses they might create through natural predation. The management plans anticipate the numbers of deer and elk that might be hunted and killed by wolves, thereby usurping the rights of humans to hunt and kill the same, pondering whether human hunters must somehow be compensated for their losses. The management plans equip each released wolf with a transmitter to track its every movement. I understand the necessity of wolf management plans if the wolf is to have any chance of survival at all in the Rocky Mountains, but the idea that humans can or even should attempt to manage an animal as beautifully wild as the wolf, as if nature were just another theme park to be carefully controlled for our amusement, rankles me.

Meanwhile, the one thing we refuse to manage is ourselves. The well-documented fact that the human species is reproducing exponentially while living in a habitat with finite resources has drawn scant attention from anyone beyond a few scientists and environmentalists who are quickly dismissed as alarmists. Some scientists estimate that in the wake of this march of humanity we are now experiencing extinction of species at a rate from one hundred to one thousand times higher than in prehuman times. And as E. O. Wilson puts it in his book *In Search of Nature,* "We have only a poor grasp of the ecosystem services by which other organisms cleanse the water, turn soil into a fertile living cover, and manufacture the very air we breathe."

The wolf provides us a perfect example of how each species we remove reverberates through the ecosystem in ways that we cannot possibly predict or correct. Research done by Utah State University shows wolf reintroduction in Yellowstone National Park has possibly led to stabilization of elk herds and an increase in grizzly bears, foxes, ravens, magpies, bald eagles, and golden eagles. And because of changed elk grazing patterns when wolves were reintroduced, it may also lead to an increase in riparian willow areas and restoration of aspen groves, which have not regenerated themselves since the 1920s, about the same time the wolves disappeared.

It seems to me that in our pursuit of happiness and the American dream—something I wholly believe in and have pursued as enthusiastically as the next person—our unchecked and unconscious extermination of other species risks degrading and destabilizing a complex support system that cannot be tilled and replanted like our backyard gardens. As far as I can see, this puts us on a path of self-destruction, and until we experience a shift of collective consciousness that allows us to find our place in the cycle of nature instead of perceiving ourselves as nature's manager, I worry we will stay on that path.

A few months ago, I walked naked in the desert. It was never my intention to do so, but a generous run of clean, red sand through slickrock seduced me to pull off hiking boots and thick wool socks. I stepped tenuously at first, then sank my left foot up to the ankle into cold sand while my right foot found the smooth stone. I was barely aware of the articles of clothing that followed the boots and socks because that's what nature does—calls forth our own human nature in its purest form. To the best of my knowledge, that sort of fusion with the natural world might be the only way to get to the core of ourselves. And I'm afraid that's what we risk losing—the essential capacity to tap into our own animal nature—if we cannot find a way to let the wild run wild.

Until then, however, we're left with wolf management plans and other small steps of redress. For the unfortunate truth is, the wolf has to play by our rules. Wolves will be allowed to survive as long as they do not encroach upon the ever-expanding territory of humans the way we have shamelessly encroached upon theirs.

Less apparent, and possibly more urgent, than the reverberations through the ecosystem are the reverberations with each loss through the collective spirit and character of humanity. And it is that—that indefinable twinge in the gut, that longing you cannot verbalize, that hard-wired human connection to what remains wild on this earth—that makes my father drop his head a little closer to the fencepost and speak softly about wolves.

Aaron Abeyta

Aaron Abeyta grew up on a sheep and cattle ranch in Colorado's San Luis Valley. He teaches at Adams State College in Alamosa and often writes about cultural, historical, and social issues common to that area. His poetry collection Colcha won the Colorado Book Award and the American Book Award. This chanting poem weaves together threads of family, fear, sheep, loss, words, his hometown of Antonito, and wolves.

I Write These Words

i write these   i write these   i write these
i write these for my town
these words are not about extinction
these words are for my brother
who rises while venus burns
these words are milk poured into bottles
these words are shadow
my town is dying my town is alive
these words are my town
my town is a wolf   these words are wolves
i write these wolves
they are shadow they are fog
these words are wolves
these words weave in   these words weave out
these wolves weave in and out of trees
these words are about salvation
these words are the only herd of sheep still up high
these words are for those
who would see my brother's sheep gone
these words are sheep emerging from the trees
i write these wolves

they are light they are dark in and out
they are invisible shadow that moves through trees
these wolves are words
that speak to a waning crescent while venus burns
i write for my town
i write for my brother who rises early
i write because
some believe that to save is to kill
i write these wolves
because my language is dying
i write these words because
someone tried to save my town
i write them i write them because
someone tried to save my town by cutting out its tongue

these wolves are lambs
these words are wolves who are also lambs
these words are a flash of silver
these words are wolves that weave
light dark shadow invisible
these wolves are a pack of words
these words are a herd of sheep
these words   all the words are fog
the earth is breathing   venus burns
my brother rises   orphan lambs cry into the morning

the air is cold
a wolf is speaking these are its words
i write these wolves as the mountain earth
breathes low fog into the morning
a wolf weaves through the breathing
sheep are made of fog
the sheep are fog flowing into a great meadow
i write them and they are fog

someone tried to save us
i write these wolves
because they began by killing us
my town is a wolf
my town is woven between three rivers

my town is sheep
my town was thousands of sheep
my town is poor   my town is rich
i write these because my town
is a wolf   i write these because
words are lost   i write these wolves
for the words that are lost
these wolves are language
these wolves weave through trees
these words are fog
these wolves are language   these wolves
are words that have been lost
the language weaves
the words are a bare thread
the words are weak
i want to save them

i write these words   i write these wolves   i write these sheep
my brother's sheep my brother's sheep are
the only herd up high
these words are a bare thread
these words i write
are a bare woolen thread
these words these words these wolves these words are fog
words these words any words
the words i write   these   that i
write here   it is a thursday   i write   on a thursday
words that are wolves

people hate me with their words
my town is broken by words
my town is broken by only one word
i write this word i write it
here   the word   the word
the wolf i write is loss

someone writes words
that hate my brother's sheep
i write these words   these
words i write are for my brother's sheep

i write wolves   the words
are wolves being saved
the words are sheep being killed
the wolves will not do the killing
what kills my brother's sheep
will be more powerful than water
words not wolves
will kill my brother's sheep

i write these   i write these
i write these wolves
these wolves are my town
these words are children with one language
these words are wolves   words   wolves
they are a pack of wolves at the edge of a great meadow
someone save something
these words are wolves
these words are venus as it burns
these wolves are children
someone save something without killing something else

i write i write i write
to someone who comes to save me
i write to someone
who would kill four hundred years
i write for those four hundred years of tradition
i write for the wolf
who was here before the tradition
these words are a bare thread
a bare woolen thread
these wolves i write are one herd up high
i write these wolves for someone
who would save me by cutting out my tongue

these wolves weave
these wolves are the barest of thread
these sheep weave   both weave
words weave wolves
weave words
sheep and wolves are woven

i write these   i write these   i write these
i write these because i am afraid
there   i've said it
these wolves are words
these words are fear
these words
are sheep   these words
are fear

someone will try and save something
their words will be fear
we kill what we fear
these words are wolves   these words are sheep
i write them both i write them both i write them both
as venus burns into thursday
i write these   i write them both
i write these   i write these
so salvation will not be a word
a wolf that sounds like loss

Laura Pritchett

Laura Pritchett, author of the award-winning collection of short stories Hell's Bottom, Colorado *and the novel* Sky Bridge, *lives in northern Colorado near the small cattle ranch where she was raised. Her essay offers a thoughtful look at the concerns of ranchers and suggests that for all of us, a richer and more balanced future will include rhetoric that matches "the heart's words."*

Sight the Gun High

He'll admit he's not the typical rancher, and five seconds in his kitchen confirms this. "Bush Must Go," reads the bumper sticker on his fridge, "Cows Not Condos," "World Peace," and "Selected Not Elected," with Bush's name crossed out. I've been in a lot of ranchers' kitchens, but not one like this, not with organic soap next to the sink, a Christmas card from John Kerry, a peace sign on the wall. And unlike other ranchers I've known, he's chatty on the phone, which rings about every five minutes—he's running for the Colorado State Senate as a Democrat—and given the political feelings out here, there's probably a lot of talking to do. While he takes one such call, I glance around his kitchen, at the wood stove keeping the room warm on this rainy fall day, the wooden floors and walls, the huge windows.

There are thirteen hundred acres of his land out there, dips and rises of meadows that border the Elk River. Close by, Red Angus bulls rest, knees folded under hulking bodies, chewing their cud, and far beyond, the pines of Routt National Forest slope upward and give way to waves of mountains. We're pretty far north here, past boutique-besieged Steamboat Springs, past the ranchettes, past the fancy houses, into country of round hay bales, pickup trucks, and horses that, invigorated by the cool fall weather, gallop across pasture.

Jay Fetcher is a lithe man in a fleece jacket, khaki hiking pants, and comfy-looking moccasin shoes, and to be honest, he looks like he belongs a little closer to town than out here. He's been ranching his whole life, though, and with an advanced degree in animal genetics and a reputation for progressive practices, he seems an interesting mix of tradition and new-school science and ideology. I figure that if any rancher were open to the possibility of ranching alongside wolves, it would be him. And he's going to be one of the first to do that, as the gray wolves migrate from Wyoming into the top portion of the state. He and his neighbors are the testing ground, basically, for wolves in northern Colorado, and I'm curious what he and others are going to do when they come.

"People aren't going to be very happy," he says calmly when I pose this question to him. "They're not. But wolves are right at the doorstep, they're coming, they're probably already here. What we do when they get here, that's the question."

I wait for him to say more, but he doesn't, so I nudge him. "And what will that be? The three Ss?"

I try to make a joke of it—this rancher lingo for "shoot, shovel, and shut up"—but he doesn't smile and he doesn't blink an eye when he says, "Yep, pretty much."

"Really?"

"Really."

"Like, how many ranchers are going to take that approach?"

"Like around Craig, about one hundred percent."

"About one hundred percent of ranchers around Craig would shoot a wolf if they saw it?"

"Yep, pretty much."

I bite my lip and look out his window. I was hoping Jay—this notoriously liberal rancher—would dispel my fears that this was true. That he, if anyone, would be optimistic enough to see a different pattern, a different take, a changing ideology. I've been asking every rancher I bump into lately what he or she thinks about wolves, and I get the familiar arguments: We worked hard to get them out of here, for a reason; Colorado is too populated; wolves roam and kill too much; it's too late to bring them back; they're just flat-out unnecessary; they're some romantic nonsense that only rich urbanites could think up; and why the hell would we want to make more trouble than we've already got? The Colorado Cattleman's Association doesn't want them. Neither does the Farm Bureau, the Colorado Wool Growers Association, or any other agricultural organization I know of. And though agriculture-based people only make up 2.5

percent of Colorado's population these days, they're the ones who will be dealing with wolves. They've got political sway, and they've definitely got guns. And there's just not a lot of support for *Canis lupus* out here, not among the ranching crowd I come into contact with.

Jay looks about as discouraged as I am. He admits he's open to wolves, under certain circumstances, but acknowledges that he's a rare duck—so I ask him how other ranchers could come around, or at least think twice before taking a shot and getting out the shovel.

And here the conversation turns a little, into something more hopeful, and we discuss real-world ways of walking this very narrow path. How to acknowledge and deal with, as he puts it, the "very tight balance."

"Here's what I want," he says, holding up a finger for each point: "1) the ability to protect my property, 2) and cattle, 3) aggressively, 4) but carefully."

Meaning this: Jay wants the right to take a shot "across the bow" at wolves that are threatening his cattle—to teach them to fear humans and their belongings—and to have this be within his legal rights. There's no doubt that wolves are going to kill livestock, and that they need to be discouraged from doing so if they're going to have a chance.

And when the wolves do kill livestock, the subsequent action is important too. The idea of ranchers being compensated for wolf-caused losses is not universally popular, to be sure. Ranchers expect compensation, arguing that wolves put their livelihood in jeopardy; opponents say that ranchers shouldn't be reimbursed for losses suffered because of Mother Nature. Plus there's the question of who's going to pay, how much, and how all that gets determined. It gets complicated. But one clear thing is that if ranchers are going to keep the guns down, they're going to want compensation for dead animals.

"Well, but you lose animals to lightning," I say.

"I can't control lightning, wolves I can," Jay says. "Look, I'm willing to put up with a few dead animals a year. Accept it as part of the bargain, part of the gamble. But more than that, no way."

And so I ask him, "In the best of all possible scenarios, how would the system work so that you—and other ranchers—would be compensated in such a way that the wolves could stay alive?"

"If I find a dead animal," Jay says, "and there's enough evidence of a wolf kill, here's what I want:

"(1) No rigmarole—I want to be compensated quickly and easily.

"(2) That compensation should not always be based on market value. What some people don't realize is that losing a cow sometimes means the loss of fifty years of genetic material—there's *a lot* more than market value at stake. There also needs to be compensation for losses and injuries. For example, I have a friend in Wyoming who had his horses chased into a fence by wolves, and they were all cut up. Wolves cause trouble, trouble that's expensive.

"(3) Local control. Twenty years ago, I could talk to the Forest Service guy about problems, now everything has to go to Washington, D.C., and it takes a year. Decisions coming out of DC are so out of touch with what locals want that it's crazy. Bring the control back home.

"(4) Trust. There needs to be trust between Division of Wildlife/Forest Service and the rancher. Right now, relations are poor. The situation always depends on the local government guy. And I don't think ranchers will claim wolf responsibility if it's not a wolf. But when they make a claim, they don't want to have to defend that claim. They want to be trusted.

"(5) And finally, if a wolf is in the act of killing one of my animals, I want to be able to take it out."

~

A rancher's primary job is to husband livestock. I grew up on a small ranch in northern Colorado, and my childhood memories are dominated by scenes of doing just that. The calf born in cold weather put into the bathtub, its blood streaming with warm water down the drain. Other calves in the kitchen, late at night, their new soft-looking hooves sliding across linoleum as they tried, by instinct, to stand. Coke bottles full of milk and newborn calves sucking, mouths wrapping around glass and plastic. Once I saw my mother, desperate to save a suffocating newborn calf, bend down and administer mouth-to-mouth resuscitation, and I watched the calf kick and come back to life. I remember my dad reaching his finger, expert and with lightning speed, into the mouth to pull out milky goop stuck in the mouth of another. I've checked on cattle with him a hundred times—counting, looking, searching for the stray, caring. I have watched his eyes as they watch, as they pay attention.

This deep-rooted care is at the core of ranching, and it goes way beyond reason or economic sense. It's an odd form of love, to be sure—fierce protectiveness for an animal that will probably be sold or slaughtered, but also the belief that while it's alive, by god, the animal is going to be guarded and nurtured.

I stop frequently at my parents' ranch these days—I ended up settling down very near the place where I was raised, and their ranch is on my way home from town. I wander in the farmhouse to play a few notes on their piano, since I don't have one; or to the garden to pick a cucumber or two;

or out back, to look at the cows. Sometimes my husband and I help with the haying, or fixing an irrigation pipe, or putting up a fence. Generally I find my parents checking cattle or tending to horses or feeding the chickens. Or they're caring for some odd creature—they've been known to have peacocks and pigeons and raccoons in the house—and there are often a stranger's horses and mules and sheep outside, since my parents' place seems to be some sort of unofficial way station for traveling animal people. My parents are like magnets to animals in need, and the only thing that would surprise me now is if I showed up and some unusual creature wasn't present.

There was a time, on this ranch, when animals were shot—fox, coyotes, rattlesnakes, prairie dogs. I grew up with guns and the idea that some animals were to be killed. But times changed, and so did my family. Hunting hasn't been allowed on the place for years. Now, when a fox eats the chickens, my parents buy new chickens, and are more careful to lock them up. When the bear tears apart the new beehives, my mom actually seems a little happy for the bear. There aren't as many guns sitting around anymore, and when they're fired, it's only at pop cans. There has been a real shift in my lifetime; every rancher I know has let go of the idea that every undomesticated creature in sight is suspect.

Wolves, though. That's a hard one. My parents probably won't need to contend with them—not in this part of the state—but the impulse I see in them, I see in other ranchers. An honest-to-god willingness to live and let live, but also a knowledge that livestock must be protected. It's a fragile balance. There's a deep need to protect, and there's a suspicion of the things that can come in and hurt.

No wonder ranchers don't embrace the wolf. A bloody dead calf is something more than a lost miscellaneous animal, or a monetary figure. The heart hurts in these cases. And how many of us open our arms up to a painful thing, ready to embrace danger? I think ranchers would like wolf proponents to understand this. Why it's so hard to welcome an animal who is, yes, gorgeous, and wild, and part of the natural balance—yes, all of those things, but a creature that's also going to break their heart a time or two.

Fascinating conversations occur on the Internet, no doubt about it. With anonymity and ease come words that shoot right out, no censorship, no discretion. I love listening, though I can't say that I love what I hear.

A quick search brings up an online debate prompted by a federal wolf agent being accused of trespassing by a rancher in Wyoming. This particular chat group has a moderator, and the conversation runs like a rowdy dinner gathering, everybody throwing in fragments, not all logical or sequential. The chat-room conversation goes something like this:

That rancher in WY should S. S. S.

What's that mean?

Shoot, shovel, shut up.

Comment Removed by Moderator.

If the rancher gets upset over seeing a stranger on his land, sounds like he is hiding something.

Maybe he's just trying to protect something. Like his cattle.

Comment Removed by Moderator.

Sounds like a juvenile pissing contest.

Rich environmental wackos have bought ranches in the West with the intention of raising predators like wolves and coyotes to drive the real ranchers off their land.

Comment Removed by Moderator.

Wolves have been seen happily ripping tails and udders off of cattle almost to the Colorado state line.

The wolves are getting fat off ranchers' calves.

I agree 100%. Make sure to cut the radio collars off and go to some truck stop with a Mexican plate on it, then throw the collars on board (should get them tracking boys in quite a tizzy). I doubt the brownshirts at USFW would understand, but ALL illegal aliens need to go, two or four footed!

Comment Removed by Moderator.

I know my land and what I have to do to protect and prolong its use. It's called stuartship [sic]. The practice that is coming into widespread use is the 'three S's.' Works for me.

Shoot, shovel and shut up is what I say.

I read on and on. There are a few thoughtful comments too, questions and philosophical enquiries, but most of the conversation is angry venting, and it makes me sad. I'm not surprised, though. I'm used to this language and this defensive, hard stance.

It's hard to understand such language in the context of love. It's almost impossible. It's hard to imagine that these are the same people that are out in the middle of the night, lugging a calf through a snowstorm, keeping it alive. But I'm telling you that they're related. This is the one thing I most want to convey: the harsh words come out of something more tender. And it comes out of feeling attacked and misunderstood.

And that goes for both sides.

For some time, I've lived in two worlds. A poetry reading one night, a Grange meeting the next. A concert to benefit the environment, then a

Cattleman's Association dance. I've heard unkind words and angry rhetoric from both groups, and I've also heard thoughtful, careful speech. In both cases, I know that most of the words come from a place of care and concern.

If we would all approach this issue with a little grace and sensitivity, maybe the rhetoric will change, and people will back down, and voices will get softer. Maybe, just maybe, the three Ss will slowly fade away. It could happen.

～

Jay is taking another phone call—he's talking politics, hoping to change some ideas—and so I have a moment to look out his window toward his ranchland. What if? What if a gray wolf's out there, running, hugging the valley, moving unseen? Thick fur dark over the back and lighter at the chest, black-tipped ears, sharp eyes, skinny legs, alert. Alive. Perhaps it's a female, and there are wolf pups growing in her belly. Perhaps it's a male and he's moving toward a kill—elk or calf or deer—and his body leaps, caught in flight, between spaces, and then there is a thud, as both prey and predator come down.

How can that happen, and ranchers survive too?

I believe ranches are one of the best ways of preserving land and ecosystems in the West. *They* are, in large part, what give the West space—and yet, an acre of Colorado's agricultural land is lost every three minutes. I'm a sentimental sort, and when I drive by a bulldozer tearing into rural land, I shake my head *no* to the tears that threaten to spill out, every time I see this land being ruined, every single time.

I eye a kitchen towel in Jay's kitchen: "Give up drinking, smoking, and fat and you'll be really healthy till you kill yourself."

Funny. And it seems to indicate that some dangers are worth it.

Like wolves, maybe. When he's off the phone, I ask him, "Okay, final question: What would you do if you saw a wolf here tomorrow?"

His eyes and body shift from explanation mode to a place that's more about his heart. He thinks for a minute and then he says, "That would be a great thing to see. I'd say 'yippee!' I'd tell authorities. And then I'd wait and see. A wolf. Well, that would be something, wouldn't it?"

～

Hope is like a campfire: it rises up, comes close to dying out, the embers wait to be rekindled. At a cattleman's dinner and dance I attend this weekend, there's a crowd gathered outside an old Grange building, and I bring up wolves again with an old acquaintance of mine, a rancher with land right at the Wyoming line. She hasn't seen any wolves, she says, but there are rumors, and she wouldn't be surprised if she saw one soon.

"And if you do?"

"Oh," she says, "Well."

"The Three Ss?"

"Well, yeah."

And then the usual: the people who want wolves are not the people who know the land. The government makes everything too difficult. Compensation is never fair. Wolves won't work.

I bite my lip and look away. There's a gorgeous sunset, full of pinks, and I keep my eye there. I've noticed that about myself—how my body and eyes orient themselves toward the mountains any time I'm feeling sad, as if there's strength for me out there in the wild. I wander toward the mountains, away from the party, and stand in the dark and listen to country music and, as the stars start to reveal themselves, I think hard about how wolves can make it here. It won't be easy, and I guess that means it's going to have to start with some maybes.

Maybe ranchers can move their cattle around more, use guard dogs and hazing devices, and even take shots "across the bow," and maybe the non-ranchers will have to trust them.

Maybe we, as consumers, will pay more attention to what we buy. There's wolf friendly beef out there, sort of like dolphin-safe tuna—a certification given to ranchers who allow wolves on their property. Maybe it's up to consumers to demand, buy, and pay more for it.

Maybe this wolf debate is much bigger, and involves a reassessment of our underlying philosophical assumptions. Maybe we need to conserve more, change our consumptive practices, and figure out what we value. Maybe there would be more room if we all quit using so much.

Maybe if ranchers weren't operating on such fragile financial margins, they could tolerate more losses. Maybe ranching is no longer a viable enterprise—and if we want it to be, we'll have to rethink current policies; and if we don't, maybe we can think up ways to protect the ranchlands of the West.

Maybe, when balance is restored, wolves will take care of the overabundant elk and deer, and the aspen and willow stands will return, and there will be more migratory birds, and more riparian vegetation for beavers, and then aquatic life will improve, and maybe this will make it all worth it, to ranchers and nonranchers alike.

Maybe a fair and friendly compensation can be worked out and employed locally and with grace.

Maybe the rhetoric can sound more like the heart's words.

And maybe, then, there can be a shift. Maybe, at that moment of aim, at that moment of decision, when breath is being held and the crosshairs on the sight find wolf, maybe that gun will move up a little, and there will be enough space, and life.

Rosa Salazar

Rosa Salazar, an MFA candidate in poetry at Colorado State University, grew up on a ranch in the San Luis Valley of southern Colorado. Describing a series of sightings in Conejos County (and quoting, in the italicized lines, from a 2003 Colorado Division of Wildlife document, "Guidelines to Gray Wolf Reports in Colorado"), she explores some of the shared territory of ranchers, farmers, and environmentalists, all people who love the land.

Sightings in Southern Colorado

if even in my dream
hoarse howl
cracks in the forest
a gray humped stone
twitches
from the stone's long nose
a body
from the stone's body
wolf

1. campsite off Highway 17 on Cumbres/
        La Manga Pass, Conejos County, Summer 2004

flashes in the distance
                        the same sound
deep howl, hollow
                        wolves in the Gila made
rusted, husky bark
                        the campfire burns out slowly
too haunting not to be

. . . *Conejos County . . . greater chance . . . wild . . . topography . . .*
        vegetation . . .

2. five miles southeast of Manassa, Los Rincones,
Colorado, Summer 2004

coyote yowls and yips
                        thin through the summer
chills at two a.m.
                        someone with a gun?
worrying about the calves
                        prairie dogs are taking over
but no coyote kills
                        we miss their sharp music
some die from hard births in snow drifts
                        we are used to them being
                            always there

. . . wolf predation on coyote . . . Yellowstone . . . changed . . . social behavior . . .

3. East of Continental Divide in southern San Juan Mountains,
      hunting season 2002

Tío Elliot's voice
a laughing whisper
                I was following a game trail through timber so thick
you couldn't see the sky. The trail curved right and we startled each
other. The wolf had been trotting down the path and it yelped, short,
sharp. I could see its big gray eyes
                he describes
bringing his gun down, the wolf leaping and bolting ten yards away.

. . . endangered . . . illegal to . . . harass . . . assessment . . .
      intent does not matter . . .

4. Los Rincones, Spring 2004

binoculars at the window
                watching the cattle
streamlined noses, pointy ears
                one would move, look around
long legs, Tío Edwin said

then another, circling
"anything with gray fur and four legs"

. . . permit would allow intentional . . .potentially injurious . . . nonlethal . . .
harassment . . .

5. Los Rincones, Summer 2004

field of miniature volcanoes
$2 per small head to the boys
to vacate, exterminate
with their .22 with a sight
empty the prairie dog holes
lying in wait on the haystack
that can break a cow's ankle
heads will emerge, sniff air

. . . statutes . . . conflict . . . $2 bounty . . . tacitly encouraging . . .
take of wolves. . .

6. intersection of Road M and Hwy 142, two miles east of Manassa,
winter 2004, 4:30 a.m.

Tía Elaine on her way back to Austin:
In the still-dark morning headlights forge a path of light. Something
moves near the stop sign. Two wolves materialize from the bushes. They
freeze in the light, the fringe of fur under their eyes as white as the
snow-packed road. Pink tongues loll out of their open mouths, clouds of
condensation forming from their breath. Their bodies, bristling immensi-
ty. I mostly remember their faces.

. . . does not intend . . . recovery plan . . . number of wolves . . .
no plans to pursue . . .

Craig Childs

Craig Childs lives in Colorado's West Elk Mountains and works as a freelance writer and commentator for National Public Radio. His numerous books include The Way Out *and* Soul of Nowhere. *Beginning with his outrage at the digital wolves in the movie* The Day After Tomorrow, *he warns us against a future made bleak by our loss of real contact with real wild animals.*

Real Wolves

A pack of wolves stalked down the hallway, peering left and right into open doors searching for prey. A faint orange glow emanated from their menacing eyes. I sat in my seat watching them, a bag of popcorn in my lap, wondering if anyone else in this movie theater noticed anything amiss. These were not real animals. Smelling human flesh, they were on the prowl in a high-budget adventure flick, their voices made into baritone growls. They looked real on the screen, utterly tangible. Every inch of them, every motion, was a computer generation, a dream of wolves brought to life.

Once upon a time we told tales about wolves. When we were a pastoral culture fending for our livestock, they were bloodthirsty beasts who deceived innocent children and killed without mercy. Gradually, killing itself became the story, burning into our memories that all wolves—in fact, all wild things—had to go. Nowadays the stories are delivered in Hollywood color. As far as any of us knew in this movie theater, these wolves were real. We were being taught how they move and breathe and think. They were dreadful creatures, nightmares. The big bad wolf was back. Who has ever seen one in the wild to know any better?

The terror that ensued on the screen was impressive—wolves rumbling and leaping, the flying of blood as they dragged a human victim across the floor by his leg. Everything was wrong, though, none of this looking like the methodical choreography of a real wolf attack. The animals were not regarding each other as they would in a pack, no deference or cooperation. Their physical gestures were snipped and pasted to call up the deepest fears of a predator. Fluid but somehow grossly mechanical, they were robots made of ones and zeros, never once having tasted meat or rested in a field of dry autumn grass. Their muscles seemed to be in the right places, but they were not moving correctly, their motions exaggerated. Their heads turned with unnatural swiftness, their sprints starting out of nowhere and reaching unrealistic speeds far too quickly. I realized that they looked like dinosaurs in the way they leapt and charged, or like little Godzillas, all of which I learned from movies.

People screamed and ran, outflanking the wolves, outsmarting them with knives and doors and ladders. Just in time, someone flung a door closed against a lunging wolf. The animal was so single-minded, so determined, that it smacked headlong into the slammed door, leaving a smear of blood and a piercing cry. The people barely escaped with their lives, finally trapping the wolves, rendering them powerless.

Sitting in the theater, I felt weakened and alone. The wolf had been annexed, stolen from me, a living creature replaced with this story vacant of everything I had ever witnessed in wild animals.

Once I saw the print of a wolf in the Yukon Territory. The near-arctic sun coursed through bony forests of black spruce and a swift river fell down through the mountains. I had dragged my canoe onto shore and was pulling it over cobbles and mud when I noticed the track. I let the canoe rest and knelt, placing one index finger into the impression of a traveling wolf. It had been set into mud, a clean hieroglyph of an animal's life. Trotting downstream at an even pace only hours earlier, the wolf had come to the water's edge where it had stopped, watching perhaps, listening, taking account of its journey. I felt richness in its track, a creature of longing and satisfaction, of fleas and a rain-soaked pelt and thoughtful instruction to its young.

And I remember a dirt road in Alaska. I paused there one morning as a wolf crossed in front of me. Without losing a step, the wolf turned and studied me for a moment. Its eyes were thoughtful, like those of another person. It trotted across the road with purpose, an articulated rhythm of paws, gray and brown fur outlining the casual movements of its muscles. It let go of me, looking ahead again, and slipped into the willow brush where it vanished.

How lucky was I to witness such a thing in my life, contact with another animal living in this world? Very lucky, as I have been many times over: sitting twenty feet from an Arctic fox, both of us motionless and alert to the sweet tundra breeze; a mountain lion's stare penetrating my bones in a ponderosa forest along the Arizona–New Mexico line; a hummingbird rescued from the greenhouse, carried in my open palm as if I were holding a living vein of emeralds; even a bull I once saw, a domestic animal turned wild in the desert of northern Mexico, that stood taut at the crest of a sand dune where it watched me with the same curious wariness I had seen in a deer, a bobcat, a caribou. These encounters are far beyond two or three dimensions. They open passages through time and emotion, through details of the animal's evolution and adaptation, the patterns of mating and migration. They give a heartening sense of not being alone, remind me I live in a world of other animals. In a meeting of eyes, a musty scent of an animal drifting through the underbrush, lies an infinite moment.

I fear that those who witness wild animals firsthand are becoming fewer and fewer, our extinction nearing. And those who know animals strictly through the eyes of imagination, through carefully planned photographs and theatrical circus bears, are becoming ever more populous. Knowledge of the subtle, wild motions of animals is becoming arcane, leaving our memory as we steadily become the sole creature to live on this planet.

I once was walking near Wall Street in Lower Manhattan when I turned a corner and saw a giant bronze bull. It was set in a median forcing head-on traffic to split around it. Frozen in the act of rearing back, it seemed prepared to attack like a massive, carnivorous beast. I approached it with a hand out, touching its snout. This was the altar of the Financial District, a golden idol of ferocity, an untamable beast. Circling it many times, tracing its knots of muscles with my fingertips, I felt as if I were face to face with the bold confusion of my own species. For a mascot we had made a monster. Watermelons of testicles were drawn tight. I gathered myself behind the heft of its right shoulder, hiding from traffic as pools of sky cupped into its bronze body.

This bull was all wrong. Its musculature and posture both suggested a hind-leg pounce, springing like a cat, which a bull cannot do. Anyone who has sat through a rodeo knows that a real bull is a trampler, kicking with its hind legs. It uses the thick-skulled butt of its head and gores with its horns. The posture of this Wall Street bull would leave a real bull helpless, its muscles tearing from overextension, bones popping from their sockets. Its horn tips were polished from the touching of millions of hands reaching to feel the great beast, to make curious contact. Having forgotten the most basic aspects of living creatures, we have again redesigned the world while lost in our own isolated musings.

I do not want to be alone, the last cruel species on earth. I ache for wild, living things: the strayed bull living along the dunes of Sonora, the wolf glancing over its shoulder as it slips into the Alaskan bush. I want bones jabbed up through the tundra. I want wind and clouds and the long light of autumn in which a wolf sits on its haunches, eyes half closed in the warmth. I want what is real.

Michelle Nijhuis

Michelle Nijhuis lives in western Colorado and is a contributing editor for High Country News. *Her freelance work has appeared in such publications as* Smithsonian, Mother Jones, Christian Science Monitor, *and* Orion. *Contrasting the suburbs with the wilderness, the easy habitat of crows with the haunts of wolves, she asks us to remember that we all "need some foreign territory at the edges of our days."*

Sleepless in Suburbia

One morning not long ago, I got up before dawn to rendezvous with a crow biologist. I stumbled out of my hotel in downtown Seattle, struggled through the thick traffic flowing toward the Boeing plant, and finally arrived in a quiet green suburb.

I soon learned that I'd ventured into some of the finest crow habitat in the world. The endless lawns full of insects, the garbage cans ripe for foraging, and the wide roads festooned with roadkill add up to pure crow heaven. My biologist guide and I chased flocks all morning, spying on the crows as they blackened landscaped lawns and cul-de-sacs. Seattle has sprawled spectacularly in recent years, and its crow population has expanded apace: tenfold over the past twenty years, and as much as 30 percent per year at present. My guide, University of Washington professor John Marzluff, was matter-of-fact. "We're creating hundreds of acres of crow habitat every single day," he told me. "We're creating habitat faster than the crows can fill it."

The humans creating this habitat—creating the lawns, the garbage, and the roadkill—aren't proud. They're annoyed. The flocks of crows in the Seattle area are so large that their rattling cries keep residents awake at night. (Some time later, I met a man who confessed to shooting at crows from his suburban bedroom window). Younger, more adventurous crows find their way into big-box stores and downtown office buildings. Seattle and its suburbs also host booming populations of coyotes, raccoons, and other habitual scavengers, likewise attracted by housing developments and their accoutrements. Coyotes, it turns out, are particularly fond of eating housecats.

When Seattle was surrounded by unbroken forests and meadows, the coyotes and the crows weren't so ill mannered. They lived relatively quietly alongside communities of songbirds, salamanders, and mammals large and small. But when humans extended their own habitats, they handed the scavengers an unbeatable advantage. The songbirds—and other species not fond of eating garbage—mostly fled the area or died, and the crows, magpies, and cockroaches began feasting with abandon.

Scavengers mirror human habits, and our own reflection is admittedly interesting, if occasionally irritating. But there's not much of the truly unexpected in the life of a crow, or a coyote, or, for that matter, a cockroach. Most of them live where we live, eat what we eat, and follow in our tracks. For deeper surprises, we need to travel beyond our own territory. We need the places not yet dominated by humans, those still ruled by wilder species.

One November in Idaho, I tagged along with a couple of wolf researchers as they tracked their study animals. In a small town in west-central Idaho, we climbed into a tiny tin can of a plane and sputtered toward the forested slopes of the Frank Church–River of No Return Wilderness. In the mid-1990s, the federal government released some thirty-five wolves from Canada into remote areas of Idaho; now, researchers estimate that more than three hundred roam the state. The Nez Perce tribe oversees the reintroduction program, hiring biologists and acting as local ambassadors for the wolves.

Though many of the wolves in Idaho wear radio collars, and the researchers carried a bulky receiver, signals were difficult to pick up. The wolves were down there somewhere, hundreds of feet below amid the snow and the pines and the firs, but they weren't eager to be seen. The landscape was so huge, its topography so full of crinkles and deep folds, that I began to think our mission was hopeless; even with the help of technology, how could we hope to find a single animal?

Finally, just as the thin air lulled me into a stupor, the receiver started to bleep, and we turned toward the signal. We banked back and forth over a low rise until one of the researchers shouted and pointed: There it was, the proverbial lone wolf, loping along the contour of that vast landscape. In a moment, the wolf was out of sight, covered by thick forest.

For the biologists, the sighting was one data point among hundreds, but all of us sat up straighter and breathed a little harder. Watching that wolf was, as you might guess, nothing like spotting a flock of crows around a garbage can, or seeing a coyote take down a housecat. We'd traveled a long way for one moment, and I felt lucky. I felt as though I'd peeked into a more distant and dangerous world, seen something of a life very different from my own. But I hadn't seen very much, and I was left with a lot more questions than answers: Where was the wolf going, and where had it been? Was its pack nearby? Did it have pups? The biologists weren't certain, though their years of research allowed them to make some good guesses. Unlike crows, wolves are not our familiars; to a great extent, their daily lives remain unknown to us.

In generations past, people were surrounded by risky, mysterious places, and many longed to subdue them. Now, as the wild world disappears, we can see that it is finite and valuable, full of endless questions. Scientists, for all their rational talk, survive on these questions, and on their intermittent glimpses of the answers. Children, forever thrilled by the strange and sublime, are really no different. All of us, in our own ways, need some foreign territory at the edges of our days. It helps hold off the crows, the coyotes, and the cockroaches. And it helps us sleep better at night.

Matthew Cooperman

Matthew Cooperman is the author of A Sacrificial Zinc *and the new chapbook* Words about James. *A founding editor of the journal* Quarter After Eight, *he teaches poetry in the MFA program at Colorado State University. This poem explores the way wolves are situated—in the wild and in our culture—as actual living creatures mysterious enough to engender a symbolic response.*

Running Wolf

with capture in its shoes, in its jaws the obverse: wild is not lewd.
Such splendor duly muted, our relationship to pulse, a fear of fur
where the hormone does not sound. "Let heat and cold reshape us
toward the land." Too much to ask?

A sited scene: mating pair, three-year-old grays. "After mounting
the female the male swivels 180 degrees while still attached. As if shy,
the two animals stand locked together for upwards of half
an hour, looking the other way." (Bateman)

Our research pending, our acronyms compounding. NEH as DOA,
NSF as MIA, these acts of the endangered brood still so
poorly understood. Such is the Way of the Hominid,
good science drinks small dollars.

Or is it simply force? A congress locked in pork. Development as
"as we can." Or the katabatic wind, the sea mount far off
rising, the migration pattern lessening.
"What is the pith of the cell?"

Population rises, extraction industries scrape off the bad bad wolf.
One gray goes down near I-70, stiffens in the wind.
"Is it a lack of space that makes us rapacious?" One could say
quite likely, though we strum a "never ending." A nerve ending.

Our "red in tooth and claw" an image of ourselves. Don't bite the mouth
that feeds, it's watching adaptation, a rhizome extension and paws
designed for snow. Each nuthatch in its sphere a real achievement.
"And we therefore remain faithful to the inspiration of the savage mind

when we recognize that, by an encounter it alone could have foreseen,
the scientific spirit in its most modern form will have contributed
to legitimize the principles of savage thought and reestablish it in
its rightful place" (Lévi-Strauss).

If we believe in complexity in thinking why not complexity in life?
The atavistic hormone leaps and links. This is as simple as it appears.

M. John Fayhee

M. John Fayhee is the publisher of the Mountain Gazette *and the author of eight books, including three coffee-table books with nature photographer John Fielder. Writing from his home in Frisco, Colorado, he rails against the softness and self-indulgence he sees around him and predicts that with the return of wolves, "our social herds will begin to thin."*

Unreal State

There it was, all over our local headlines, the surprise inevitable: Wolf killed on Interstate 70, last year, just a few miles from where these words are being penned. I mean, a goddamned wolf! First reaction was to say, well, of course a wolf was killed on I-70. Everything with four legs eventually gets killed on I-70, a section of asphalt sanctimoniously considered by people who give a shit about this sort of thing to be the very lifeblood of the part of Colorado—the real estate resort part—that economically relies upon the millions of vehicles that annually make the recreational pilgrimage from the flatlands to the mountains and, thankgodfully, back.

I-70 is actually as much of a rabbitproof fence as it is a transportation corridor; it serves as one of the more egregious examples of habitat fragmentation known to humankind. There is not one single place where wildlife migrating, or, hell, just taking a stroll, can cross that wretched Interstate without having to jump a limited-access fence, cross two lanes of frenzied roadscape, cross a median, cross another two lanes of frenzied roadscape, then jump another limited-access fence.

There used to be one wildlife migration land bridge (though it was marked as such on no map I know, meaning the animals had to sniff it out for themselves), artificial though it was, where I-70 goes under the Continental Divide via the Eisenhower Tunnel. But, in the late 1990s, in an act that showed you don't have to be Vail Resorts or Intrawest to screw the natural world up, Loveland Ski Area erected a lift just about atop the Divide, almost in the middle of that one last migration corridor. So, even that one last safety zone was sullied, though the Powers That Be at Loveland were very quick to point out, as ski area flaks are genetically predisposed to do, that they were under the belief (armed as they were with a Forest Service study that was completed in about eleven seconds) that the new lift would not affect migrating wildlife one whit, and, even if it did, tough noogies for the deer and the elk, because the ski industry has become so competitive that, without additional available terrain, the little areas such as Loveland will just wither away.

And all of us who hang our hats in Colorado know full well that economic arguments, even inane economic arguments, trump not only all other arguments but sanity as well. This is not a state that was settled by pilgrims searching for the promised land, no matter what that land might hold; rather, it is a state that, clear back to the Jeremiah Johnson trapper types, was populated by people looking for fiscal burning bushes, and the pox on all that has ever come or ever will come, between the residents of Colorado and their entitled rewards.

The reaction to the wolf's Interstate 70 death was predictable here in Colorado, a state that prides itself on the delusion that this is still fundamentally a wild place. The reaction was: See. Told ya. What we have been told is that Colorado ain't Alaska or even Montana, that Colorado is too densely populated, that it lacks the trackless areas necessary to sustain populations of large carnivores like grizzlies and wolves and maybe even lynxes. Even those sporting Sierra Club bumper stickers on their Outbacks lamented the news of that one wolf's demise—much as it would be nice to have lobos running wild through our state, maybe it's just not feasible in the early twenty-first century. If the one single wolf that has passed through Colorado in who-knows-how-many years managed to get smooshed on I-70, how many would meet a similar fate if the species was actually reintroduced?

This is a state populated by folks who think they're tough because they ski The Basin and climb fourteeners. But, as soon as there's news of a few poodle disappearances in mountain lion country—which pretty much covers (or at least used to cover) every square inch between the Front Range and the Utah border—then people start sweating and showing their true fearful colors by calling the Division of Wildlife and demanding that Something Be Done, even though it was they and their damned poodles who decided to move into lion country in the first place. The notion of falling on a ski run or having to dodge lightning bolts while bagging yet another basically benign peak is one thing; the thought that there are actually critters roaming our mountains with monster canines and an appetite for flesh is not what the New Colorado is all about.

The new Colorado is all about image; it is not about reality. I mean, look at the average person now moving lock, stock, and barrel to the High Country. I live in the heart of the High Country, so I know: These new residents (called "amenities migrants") complain loudly if the goddamned streets are not plowed down to asphalt before first light after a nightlong snowstorm so they don't have to navigate their SUVs through snowbanks on their way to Copper Mountain. They argue that towns need to regulate landscaping to make certain all yards uniformly portray the "mountain town image," even though most of these people wouldn't know a real mountain town if it walked up and bit them on the ass, wolflike. They attend town council meetings and, straight-faced, maintain how aesthetically important it is that firewood only be allowed to be stacked in backyards, so as not to visually contaminate the mountain-town image. There are two things and two things only that matter, policywise, in the Colorado mountains any more: image and maintenance of property values, even though both are interrelated illusions promulgated by the weakest of our human herd.

And neither of those illusions includes wolves running through our mountains, which are, when you get right down to it, merely one more recreational amenity to the New Coloradans, like recreation centers with creeks, art galleries with living aspens. Dioramas with the occasional biting insect. That wolves were once here is enough in the New Colorado. Surely there are, or will be, exclusive gated communities with names like Wolf Run, located in places so long cleared of wolves that you can't even hear the echoes of the ghost howls any more.

There is little doubt in my mind that one of the main reasons people choose to move to Colorado instead of Montana or Alaska is that we are, relatively, free of large carnivores. We are Wild Lite. It is easy for those of us who place environmental bumper stickers upon our pickup trucks to decry the systematic, state-sanctioned, large-carnivore holocaust that has pretty much defined not just Colorado but the entire West for more than a century. You know: "blame the ranchers." We shake our noggins and rhetorically ask how it could have been so. Then we go bag a few more fourteeners safe in the knowledge that the chances of getting attacked and eaten here in the heart of the Rocky Mountain High are virtually nil. Sure, there are signs posted near Grand Lake about not hiking by yourself or letting your child get out of sight because of mountain lion danger. There was, after all, an eight-year-old child killed by a mountain lion a couple of years back. And there was that young man, likewise, killed by a mountain lion near Idaho Springs while he was running. But we know those circumstances, tragic through they were, are anomalies. And, besides, we know full well that packs of wolves are reclusive and that they feed on weak, old, and sick ungulates, making the herds of elk and deer that swarm through our mountains stronger in the long run. These things we know.

Or do we? If wolves are reintroduced into Colorado, I believe things will change. There will be a different psychic dynamic at work when we go about the serious business of playing in these mountains. We will hear the distant howling and hike closer together. We will fidget a bit as we make our way through thick undergrowth. We will sleep fitfully in our little three-pound tents. No matter that we mentally recite mantras that the wolves will harm neither us nor ours, our sweat will be a tad more acrid as we hike next to streams loud enough to muffle the sound of approach. And this benign state, a place where lifestyle surety is all but guaranteed, where the roads are plowed down to asphalt, where the property values always rise, will be forever transmogrified. And many people will not like it. These mountains will again become something more than postcard backdrops or components of investment portfolios. They will regain something of their old Wild, even if that Wild is, when you get right down to it, as artificial as it ever was.

But, hell, manipulated Wild is likely better than no Wild.

And maybe, when the wolves start roaming close to our homes, when we start hearing their howls as we huddle before our hearths, not just when we travel into the backcountry, then maybe the genetic wiring we all share will kick in and our social herds will begin to thin. Maybe the pudgy white-legged people will stop puttering in their bluegrass lawns long enough to begin to understand that the Rocky Mountains are not their place, that they do not want to dwell where the mountains are more than postcards and amenities. Maybe they will Go Home. To Ohio or Georgia. Because, here's the thing: When that wolf got killed on Interstate 70, a True Message, a communiqué from the Deep World, was sent loud and clear: That wolf was not brought here in the back of a truck by some U.S. Fish & Wildlife team, drugged, scared, and disoriented. It made it here by itself. Like wolves and bears have done in the North Woods. Like the jaguar has done in Cochise County, Arizona. Like the grizzly may be doing in Gila country.

We think we control Wild. Wild controls itself. The wolves are coming, one way or another, and if that frightens you, good. You may fight back, as humankind always has. You may demand that wildlife regulators come in and save you and your goddamned household pets, despite the fact that it was you who opted to move to the places where true Wild once existed, and will exist again. You may buy a gun, in case Wild decides to pay you a close-encounter-type visit. You may lobby against predator reintroductions. While lobbying, you may lie, or exaggerate, or repeat the lies and exaggerations of others. But it doesn't matter. Our herd is weak. And the predators are coming back to cull us, even if that culling is conceptual. Arm yourselves. Huddle together around the fire.

The predators are coming. Their howls are even now echoing through the mountains, carried on the cold wind down the valleys, into the heart of our covenanted real estate developments, our faux fortresses, our delusions of conquest.

B. Frank

B. Frank lives in the San Juan Mountains of southwestern Colorado, has worked as a guide in the Rockies and Canyon Country for a couple of decades, publishes in the Mountain Gazette *and elsewhere, and is working on a novel of death, love, revolution, and wolves. Here he thinks about the advantages of realistic fear.*

Going Feral

I've never seen a wild wolf. Now, that's not to say I don't know how to eat like a wolf of the Arctic tundra, courtesy of Farley Mowat's self-experimentation. I can debunk wolf myths chapter and verse, using Barry Lopez's *Of Wolves and Men* as hymnal. I even vicariously danced with a spavined wolf in a motel room this summer, watching Kevin Costner's romanticized "white man goes feral" flick again on cable TV, as an alternative to CNN's fearmongering song and dance. Yeah, I know what wolves look like. Hell, I've got fifteen months worth of portraits on a calendar I bought after some bastard stole my last one as I recreated peaceably on our public lands not long ago. The wolf models howl, nuzzle their young, and stare back at me like Playboy models with fur. Most of these photos were likely shot in a "wildlife park" (a type of zoo without cages), in which samples of incorrigibly wild species are sentenced to spend their lives and hit poses for the cameras. Ms. September peers from between two aspen trees; perfect ears, nose, and fur are lighted beautifully. One eye is exposed, and looking into it makes me wonder what they see in us as we debate their right to exist in the margins of the swath of devastation we euphemistically call society.

I have heard wolf howls on the north rim of the Grand Canyon, albeit from the lips of a park ranger we used to call the Wolfman. He did the evening talk in the historic North Rim Lodge. The hotel was built in the 1930s, just a few years after the Wolfman's ranger predecessors hunted the last wolf out of the lush aspen, fir, and pine forests of the Kaibab Plateau. They shot all the wolves while espousing a belief that those "ravenous predators" were to blame for decreasing deer herds, meanwhile ignoring that humans were decimating herds across the west by destroying habitat with rampant logging and grazing, and then using improved weaponry to collect trophies of their attempts to go back to the "wilds" they had just destroyed. (Fans of Teddy Roosevelt may now leave the room.) The Wolfman told us that the plateau's deer herds did in fact increase after the wolves were gone, until overpopulation and drought combined to cause the first of many population crashes. By the late 1980s, all science pointed to the need for predators in a healthy ecosystem, and the Wolfman was doing his nightly best to sing the reintroduction gospel to the masses of park visitors.

Listening to him, I thought of another herd in need of thinning. In the early 1980s, I used to take people into the Tetons and Yellowstone country, trying to get them to venture past geysers and crowds and into the landscape. I also spent a lot of time there listening to people lament the "problem" of starving elk on the flats of Jackson Hole every winter. Feeding programs were holding off the "disaster" of a massive elk die-off, and the herds kept increasing because of heroic human efforts. I'd puzzled over the hand-wringing, and then thrown up my own hands in despair that humans would ever see the light and reintroduce natural predation to balance the herds. My despair was proven unwarranted, because even as the Wolfman preached at us on the North Rim, wolves were being trapped in Canada, transported to the Yellowstone country and sicced onto the herds. We should all know the story by now; but the short version is, "It works."

Talking up the Wolfman's ideas to my own little herds of feral wannabes as we walked the rims and interior of the Grand Canyon, I learned firsthand of the vestigial fear that the mere thought of "wolf," out there just beyond the reach of headlamp and campfire, can inspire. A good way to terrorize your charges is to talk wolf science, then go off to your tent. After an hour or so, creep out into the night, rustle the underbrush a bit, and then—a low howl. It works every time, and guarantees an early start next morning, the better to beat the heat on those summertime hike-out days.

Fear is a good tool, used by prey species to teach their young to watch their backsides. I've tried to instill fear of certain things in my own son, watched in satisfaction as innocence was replaced by caution, and always wondered a little if I'd made him fear nonexistent danger. My self-justification is that, with access to the accurate information, humans are able to unlearn false fear. This is part of the value of wolf reintroduction experiments. No humans have been attacked by ravening wolves in the re-wolfed

Yellowstone country, and elk and deer herds are getting healthier; yet the North Rim of the Grand Canyon is still dependent on Ranger programs and twisted guide humor for wolf howls.

Down closer to my current neck of the woods, the only wolf reintroduction tried in recent years sputters along in the Gila country of the Arizona–New Mexico border. This effort sputters because local folks trot out anecdotes of wolf-killed calves and family pets, and a few fearful guntoters keep killing the wild ones every time they get a clear shot. I'm hoping to live long enough to see that situation change, and to hear wolves howling some night on my home range just north in the mountains of Colorado.

Not long ago I walked up the side of one of these mountains with a dog and a particular young lady of my acquaintance for company. One side of the mountain faces a world-class ski resort, with its attendant gaggle of peak-baggers, speed-hikers, mountain-bikers, and assorted wilderness lovers. The other side is accorded official Wilderness status and doesn't allow motors or wheels. There are no signs, no trailhead restrooms, and no (gasp) cell-phone coverage. It is, in short, about as wild as you can get in an overly "multiple-used" state like Colorado. We left the trail at timberline, bushwhacked our way to a game trail that took us into a little valley fed by a snowmelt stream, and pitched a tent that looks like a rock from a distance.

The first evening, an elk herd watched us from a ridge while we cooked our dinner and zipped ourselves into our rock. Just after dark, a cow elk came near, ears tilted forward to gauge our danger. We kept the dog still and watched through our window, while the elk walked into the open, crossed the meadow, and climbed the opposite ridge. Soon more cows and a few calves followed. They eyed our tent, then grazed a bit of meadow grass, drank some water, and disappeared into the forest. We kept still again—but I'm thinking now that I should've howled like a wolf and released the dog (though her big red body more closely resembles a fox on steroids).

During the next week, we watched the elk move along a ridge above our camp. They used the east face for morning warmth, and then moved to the valley floors and forest in the heat of day. One day, a calf got separated from the rest, and we watched a timeless drama play out from our now ignored "rock." The mother bawled several times, but the calf ignored the call. By the time the calf wanted her, the mama cow had given up and followed the herd into the forest. The calf searched about the trails for a while, then spent a solo day on the ridge. Come night, she was still there.

Next morning, after the herd trooped by on its daily trek, we investigated the slope and found no signs of a kill site. I didn't expect one, since wolves are long gone from Colorado, killed off by the same belief system that once doomed the wolf packs of the Kaibab Plateau and the Yellowstone country. Best I could tell, the calf survived her lack of caution and can pass that trait along to her progeny. Caution used to be a required survival skill for a prey species like elk, but without wolves to back it up, it's little wonder the elk youth are ignoring their elders. How many generations will it take before Colorado's elk herds are little more than residents of a large "wildlife park" zoo, caged in by McMansion subdivisions? Maybe if we'd all just go out and howl at the herds from inside our tents, we could throw a little healthy fear back into the elk; but I'd rather know there's a wolf pack in the neighborhood, pruning the herd and teaching survival skills to the hunted.

Another young "calf" wandered from his herd on the mountain that week. As my partner and I left the trailhead for our "back to the wild" adventure, a vehicle pulled up. The local search and rescue squad had received a cell-phone call from a group of hikers, reporting a missing kid. The searcher asked us to be on the lookout for him. Through that first afternoon, planes searched the mountainside. By night they had stopped, and I hope they found the kid to be okay; but over the next days I thought about our society's concern over his situation and compared it with an anecdote from my own life. As the son of divorced parents, my son returned from school to an empty house for too much of his young life. As a noncustodial parent, I was unable to engage the interest of the "proper authorities" in the situation, so I had to rely on my son's own sense of survival behavior. He was lucky, stayed to himself and out of trouble, and made it to adulthood mostly unscathed.

But too many of our society's young learn to survive by hanging out in packs of other kids with not much to do except watch "action" movies and play video games that glorify antisocial behaviors. When some of them get in trouble, we wonder in hushed tones just why the kids went wrong. Then we demand they all be locked into "educational" institutions, to be searched for weapons and bombarded by jingoistic rhetoric from recruiters for the latest War on _____ (fill in the blank with your own favorite fear). Better we should get them lost for a while in a landscape populated by a healthy ecosystem for a little real education. Even if that kid had spent a night out on a mountain listening to wolves and feeling their eyes everywhere in the darkness, nothing would have eaten him except his vestigial false fear (Barry Lopez referred to it as "theriophobia"—literally, a fear of the beast—based in superstitious beliefs), which is reinforced by fearmongers of every stripe.

Virulent resistance to bringing wolves back to their rightful homes lingers across the west. It's expressed in fears of being economically ruined (decrying wolf predation on his ranch, Teddy Roosevelt described wolves as "the beast of waste and desolation") and fear of reduced hunting opportunities (a debate that cropped up again this year in the Yellowstone country); but often it's based on theriophobia. A few years ago, the movie *Silence of the Lambs* thrilled and scared the pants off throngs of audiences, and I could toddle down to my local Super Wally World today and buy a book called *In the Name of the Wolf.* Though apparently unrelated to wolves in the west, both describe fears of "the wild beast," and other examples of popular entertainment exploiting this fear are easy to find. Since wolves epitomize "the wild beast" in human mythology, all such works make wolf reintroduction more difficult, because the retelling of a myth evokes the fears it describes. Real economic and hunting-based fears are fairly easy to counteract with compensation guarantees and scientific data, but theriophobia is a tough nut to crack. In my little corner of the world, the authorities recently changed the number of a federal highway. Why? Well, it was US 666 ("sign of the beast" in one belief system); now it's the innocent-sounding US 491. Maybe we should rename wolves something innocuous—call them poodles, for instance.

I can look at a piece of the highway formerly known as 666 from atop my home range to remind myself that theriophobia is a powerful force. The road stretches south to the Gila country, where the San Carlos and White Mountain Apache Nations have now welcomed wolf reintroduction. For many generations, tribal beliefs have venerated the presence of wolves in the landscape; and I now have high hopes that there will be a viable wild population there during my lifetime. To get wolves into Colorado, we'll have to deal with a lot of this vestigial false fear. When debating reintroduction here, I'll find myself facing arguments that evoke images of economic ruin, decimated elk herds, and Little Red Riding Hood. I'll respond by quoting Mowat, Lopez, and the ever-growing body of scientific evidence. I'll also preach that we can learn a few survival skills from having wolves in the margins of our society, because I hope to sit with my son in a rocklike tent on that mountain some night, watching a wolf pack course through a high meadow fed by snowmelt streams and a wary elk herd. When that night comes, I'll howl softly in tribute to the Wolfman and all the other wolf advocates, for putting some "wild beast" back into the landscapes of our feral adventuring.

Jack Martin

Jack Martin has been a professional river guide, a standup comic, and the recipient of a Colorado Council of the Arts fellowship. Author of the chapbook Weekend Sentences, *he lives in Fort Collins and teaches high school in Arvada, Colorado. Exploring the way ancient words like "crying wolf" keep old responses alive, this poem opens up spaces for us to think and suggests that a pack of real wolves would be a relief.*

Pack

Wolf needs wolf.

Some things should be removed from the world.

                        (Go ahead. Decide.)

A boy cries, "Wolf!"
The town rushes to his aid.
               (What would we do without this kind of peril
to unite us?)   Like wolves,

        we travel in packs.

The town says,
        "DON'T CRY 'WOLF!'"
The town lights up
as it walks away.

Of course, the boy cries again,
        "Wolf!"

(Who doesn't love attention?)

(Look at me, what I've written.)

Maybe this is why the boy cries,
again and again.
                              It is too beautiful,
this approaching. First one,
then another and another.

                    Even to think it.

          In this world that happens so slowly,
          wouldn't a pack of wolves be a relief?

                         Or a whole town lit.

So much more than unexpected.
Eyes like blue wheels,
all of them working together.

The Voltage of Legends

As anyone involved in reintroduction efforts will say, the debate about wolves is very little about the actual animals and very much about the power of culture: our conscious and subconscious images, the stories we tell ourselves and each other about wolves. Every culture gives its own meanings to the animals that surround us, and Western European culture has both revered and feared wolves, telling us sometimes about the two boys nurtured by wolves who grew up to found the city of Rome but much more often about the ravening beasts that attacked Little Red Riding Hood, wait at the door of poverty, and tried their best to eat the Three Little Pigs. The poems and essays in this section explore our rich cultural image bank and propose alternative ways of imagining and understanding these animals that will allow us all to share the land.

Steve Miles

Steve Miles grew up in Las Animas, Colorado, has an MFA in poetry from Colorado State University, makes striking clay pots, and teaches high school English in Denver. This poem explores the swirling, drifting lexicon of images and metaphors that attach to wolves.

lupus

the voltage
    of legends
        lathers
her muzzle
    tilting
        to measure
musk from air
    a slim
        beware
& a throat
    full of scree
        a communist
notion
    scavenging
        scarcity
wearing
    a blizzard
        on her shoulders
her tail
    is a snarl
        of twined

serpents
    dusting
        the opened
guts of ice
    her teeth
        are glacial
grinding
    a lexicon
        of dark
discretion
    down the boreal
        watershed
saying everything
    not suffered
        through
to the end
    will capsize
        the skies
the way black
    running paws
        lift light
from leaves
    in a finespun flu
        a frozen sigh
a lucifer cry
    that conjures
        the dew

Clarissa Pinkola Estés

Clarissa Pinkola Estés, author of the celebrated book Women Who Run with the Wolves, *lived in the woodlands of the northern Midwest as a child where she came to see the wolf as a psychic companion. A Jungian analyst and cultural anthropologist, she considers some of the ways in which thinking about wolves and wild nature can help us think about our lives and our selves. She lives in the Denver area.*

Wild Wolf—Wild Soul

I grew up in the backwoods where far to the north there were wolf packs—quite unlike the absurdist commercial the GOP ran days before the 2004 presidential election featuring what appeared to be not real wolves, but overdomesticated hybrid "wolf-dogs." The ad attempted to symbolically point out what would happen to the nation if Democrats were elected. Intentionally or not, the commercial makers vilified a creature who has, in reality, such companionability, such family values, such a conserving way of life.

But, irony of ironies, the wolf-dogs, at least to those who have ever observed real wolves, could only be seen as good actors if you considered them comedians. In the commercial, instead of leaping from their perches on powerful haunches as real wolves who are fierce creatures would, the wolf-dogs rather floppily and hesitantly hopped down from their perches like happy trained seals. Their pelts had no burrs, no straws. Their paws were clean.

No doubt some viewers imagined the offstage best boys might be holding out some Purina Dog Chow in order to cause this conflagration of smiling wolf-dogs. But, if they were real wolves, the stagehands would somehow have had to get their hands on some nice tasty lure, like mouse corpses, as that would please the greater appetite of most real wolves on most real days in most real countrysides.

When I was young long long ago, anyone encountering wild wolves in the early morning, as fog filled the cathedral trees and the fern forests, could see that they were, as we sometimes call them, *los ángeles tímidos,* timid angels, who would step around so gently and peer out at the lone humans walking through the green. It was from those observations that I saw how humans and wolves have many of the same characteristics.

And so, in one of my books, *Women Who Run with the Wolves,* a compendium of legendary tales about the deepest inner soul life that matters, I chose the wolf as the royal metaphor. I noted that women and wolves had been tarred similarly. They are often portrayed as having unending appetites, when in fact they wish only for respect, and to be allowed to follow their very great gifts in peace.

It is clear to my greater mind—the one that can see between the worlds, and hold all as having certain validities—that wildlife and the wild soul are both endangered species in our time. Over our time on earth, the soul and Nature have been looted and driven back by any number of factors in the popular culture. That once free soulful territory, whether without or within, was then overbuilt in absurdist and/or destructive ways. For long periods in our culture, the soul, like the wildlands and wildlife, has been mismanaged. The natural cycles of depth, learning, and realization of the necessity for soulful consideration in all aspects of life have too often, instead, been forced into unnatural shapes and rhythms to please the least conscious desires of self and others.

It is not by accident that the pristine wilderness of our planet disappears as the understanding of our own wild and soulful natures fades. It is not such a mystery that wolves and forests and coyotes and bears and the wild soul all have similar reputations. They all share related instinctual archetypes. As such, they are innately wise, enduring, and bold, contrary to the views of those who see such beauty as wrong, inconvenient, or simply irrelevant to their purposes. There has been an arrhythmia in the heartbeat of the cultural psyche . . . one that leaks the idea that it is all right to bypass deep thought and instead prey upon the soul that exists in all things.

The soul, like the wolf, has been erroneously reputed to be ungracious, innately dangerous, and ravenous for any form of life. But the natural instinctive psyche is wise and measured, and it is the quintessential inspiratrice. It is good, not bad, for us to study the wiser aspects of Nature when we have forgotten our own. As a poet and synesthete regarding words and images, I feel certain that art and Nature are the ways through which the soul communicates its highest values and beauties to us and to the world. Without art, without Nature and its beauty, we starve to death psychically. We sever the arteries that bring soul into the world. We become soulless.

What is outside in Nature is also inside in human nature—whether it be large rolling storms, Icelandic meadows flowering in a sudden spring, or underground artesian wells. All these are inside us in some way. It appears that to destroy living beings in Nature is also to cause Nature's resonant images and analogies to fade within the human psyche as well. It seems almost as though Nature not only creates itself—it also, in some needed and significant way, creates a heartfelt cohesion of spirit in us too—one that is awakened by finding, loving, and sheltering the soul in all things.

As a poet in the schools, I have noted that children sometimes do not know of bears and tigers and wolves any longer. If they know of these creatures of God, it is often only because they once saw a poor bedraggled animal performing lampshade-on-head tricks in a debilitating circus. The spirits of children are the poorer for this, because all of the bear, all of the tiger, all of the wolf, all of Nature, have their psychic doppelgangers in us. Without the creatures in Nature that so deeply influence our night and day dreams, that so deeply teach the psyche about spirit and endurance, about fierceness and eros, that so deeply shatter our day-to-day chitin and bring us life-giving awe, we will, as it is said in fairytales, "be made so poor we will not even have a bird to tweet at us."

Over the last thirty-five years as a practicing psychoanalyst who has listened to thousands of dreams, I have noted that children nowadays, in particular, dream less about the creatures of Nature. As Nature in our time has suffered to be burned down, bulldozed, and eradicated, the dreams of the people are changing. Whereas children used to dream bear, wolf, tiger as both friends and foes, now so many children are dreaming Machine: gigantic stomping splints and walking piers of glittering mutant metal.

I am a quintessential rationalist and face reality square on. I know from six decades of experience several somethings with certainty: It is never too late to save the dream life. It is not too late to save the soul—the individual soul and the soul of the world. It is not too late to shelter the lives of creatures and their great beauty and contributions to our planet and to our lives. The means are different from what we ever imagined, but the means exist and are intact. There is not one way, but many ways.

There is a Billie Holiday song that was covered by the great Aretha. It is called "Crazy He Calls Me." I sometimes play it on my way out to mission when winter whiteout storms roll over the Rockies where I live and eradicate everything from sight so that many souls will soon be in need. I interpret that the song tells about moving mountains if He wants them out of the way; that some people will say this is crazy, but they don't know that the soul is crazy in love, and that it'll do the difficult right away, and "the impossible will take a little while" longer. This song is one of my strongest prayers.

The other is a mere one line from a powerful prayer/poem called "Manifesto: The Mad Farmer Liberation Front" from the book *The Country of Marriage,* by Wendell Berry, a poem given me by a sister in spirit, Marilyn Auer. The poem is a long list of all the things that are perils to the heart and mind, and how to avoid injury, and even though you may be taken down, to get back up, for the last line of the poem is *"Practice resurrection."* I have it in my bones that there are many many ways to practice resurrection, and in ways that no one can prevent. The rebirth of spirit. The renewal of an ideal. The refurbishing of one's own fierce calling on this earth. Most often the hints for the why, wherefore, and how-to of resurrection come to us in dreams. All the more reason to preserve the precious headwaters that flow through the soul to inform dreams: Nature.

In my written work, I created an anthem about wolves, the most maligned image in our culture in addition to the human soul. And so, if one were to live one's life with integrity and cohesiveness, with some heart-shattering love to make a wider and deeper room, and with wisdom, I would offer humbly, one could hardly do better than this:

General Wolf Rules for Life
1. Eat
2. Rest
3. Rove in between
4. Render loyalty
5. Love the children
6. Gambol in moonlight
7. Tune your ears
8. Attend to the bones
9. Make love
10. Howl often and deeply, for as the poet Charles Simic once wrote, "He who cannot howl, will never find his pack. . ."

May we all ever find and live these essentials. May we all ever recognize and remain the recipients and protectors of the unending forms of Soul in our most fragile and fiercely made world.

Mary Sojourner

Mary Sojourner's books include Solace: Rituals of Loss and Desire *and* Bonelight: Ruin and Grace in the New Southwest. *She lives near Flagstaff, Arizona. Taking issue with the way we sometimes turn wolves into fetishes, she imagines the sharp critique a wolf might make of our current ways of living on the land.*

Bones

Sift the desert and see what you can find. It is the only work we have to do. You wish psychoanalytic advice? Go gather bones. —Clarissa Pinkola Estés

Leave the bones. They are my bones. They will never be yours. Believe what you will: that you run with me; that the turquoise Zuni hunting fetish carved in my shape gives you power; that the mask you made in the workshop in Santa Fe expresses the part of you that will someday burst free. I know a harder Truth.

You do not know me. I am not wolf. I am More. And all your efforts to know me are futile as long as you continue on your present course. You know.

You do not want to know.

My bones speak. From the Yaak, from the Mojave, from the places that have, as yet, no names; and from the places your species persists in believing it can name: Forest Highlands Meadow Clubhouse, Quail Ridge Retirement Community, Pine Canyon, Coyote Spring, Wolf Hollow Mall. My bones laugh. We rename: Slashed Forest Bulldozed Highlands Buried Meadow; Shotgunned Quail; Logged Pine Trashed Canyon; Trapped Coyote Drained Spring; Skinned Wolf Dynamited Hollow Maul.

My bones hold a workshop and make masks. See mine: white as ash, bloated, the good-boy haircut, the mouth twisted in a rictus of what is to be taken as sincerity.

My bones carve fetishes. Two humans bound with sinew. The larger holds a builder's plan. Come close. Read the specs: eight thousand square feet. Four-car garage. Indigenous landscaping!! Solar power!! We laugh. The homes—our homes—on which you humans build your houses need no landscaping. Sun and moon light our way. We laugh and you wonder if you hear the dead howl.

You do. The Dead and the Living. The Going-to-Rot and the Being-Born. Eroding sandstone and wind eroding ancient rock. Hungry hawk, hungry rabbit, voracious grass sucking nutrients and water. The ululation of a Web that has no mercy, only indigenous power. The Web that traps us all . . .

. . . and releases.

You know. You do not want to know. My bones tell you to leave us where you find us. We tell you to find your place in the web. This is dangerous work. You will be stripped down. Your bones will understand what it is to let go.

Let go.

How to let go.

This last knowledge is what we know that makes you plead for ignorance.

So be it. If that is your choice, listen no further.

You have remained. You have threaded yourself into the Greater Web. You believe that bones speak. You are here to listen.

Money. We will tell you what we know of money.

Possessions. We will tell you what we know of possessions.

Security. We will tell you what we know of security.

Time. We will tell you what we know of Time.

Money and possessions will not secure you. You will become bones.

Your efforts to avoid that knowledge; your misguided faith in money, in possessions; your illusion of security have torn the web—perhaps beyond repair. You have lost your place—perhaps beyond repatriation. We—rabbit and hawk, wolf and lichen, limestone and parasite—are no longer your neighbors—perhaps beyond reunion.

Every penny you give a global corporation kills one of us; every dollar you spend for something you don't need annihilates our home, Our Home. If you buy books in Barnes and Noble, in Borders, on Amazon.com, in Sam's Club, in Costco, you catch yourself in a leghold trap. If you save three dollars in Home Depot, you eat poisoned bait. If you own an SUV, a mini-van, buy a new vehicle every year, you gutshoot yourself; if you look back, you will see your own blood trail.

This is what we know of Time. It is Time for your species to Stop.

You know. You do not want to know.

What is left to do, to put off the Stopping? What conference needs to be held? What research needs to be done? What lie haven't you told yourself—about your needs, your wants, your inability to do without? What bones haven't you uncovered?

Here is the last research. Look in your mirror. You wear a mask. Take it off.

What do you see?

Bones.

Bones.

Bones.

Eye sockets staring back. Eye sockets that might well be wolf or crow or rabbit. Eye sockets that hold the future. Eye sockets into which you look and see one word: *Stop.*

Pamela Uschuck

Pamela Uschuk's latest book of poems is Scattered Risks. *The director of Salem College's Center for Women Writers, she lives in southwestern Colorado with two wolf-dogs. This poem, "Lecture," talks about our need for better knowledge and new imaginings of wild wolves.*

Wolf Lecture

There is the yellow about the eyes,
the impeccable reading of night
between trees, the will to shift
directions with a flick of the dew claws, rake
of leather paws on ice packed blue by the moon, even
when the belly is empty
and blood carries the wind.
      What is wilderness without the beast
and its nations of mystery?
      How do you lecture on magic
when the magician has watched you
for centuries destroy the stage?
Tonight we gather in a pack
to learn about packs, from slides
of wild wolves, their family affections
and invented games, the way
their shadows ghost across snow.
Houdinis of wilderness, they hunt
and we hear the adrenaline slam
of the stalking heart
beating our own pulses wild

while the auditorium walls
sizzle into Denali's treeless peaks,
the pine and spruce forest
dappling its slopes,
through which the wolves lope,
long-boned and easy
in their beautiful coats
before the show ends and
they disappear, gut shot by our history.

Greer Chesher

Greer Chesher writes from southern Utah and has published five books of nonfiction, including Heart of the Desert Wild, *winner of the Utah Book Award for nonfiction. This essay takes place in England, where she visits some of the traces of an ancient English vision of the wolf as guardian and calls us to preserve and restore the wild.*

A Testimony of Wolves

Devon's cold February rain pelts the still green but soggy fields of England as I trudge the footpath from Dartington toward Totnes. Mist rises from the black-and-white-patched milk cows as they watch my progress down the farm lane and onto the road. A hawk flows along the abandoned hedgerow's tall trees. I head for the forest, a few treed acres bordering the valley road to Totnes along the mill trace. From the top of the hill I see the flume's waters rushing below and the footpath hard by its side. The mud is deep on the old road between field and forest but I walk to the spring that bubbles up in an old stone well and spills over, trailing through the field's thick peat.

Turning into the forest, I find the ruins quickly. In town, people stare blankly when I ask about the old stone walls with their immense arched but empty windows. But I know the tree. Nearby, an old oak, far larger than any tree in the forest, stands alone by the place, silent, and in this early spring, leafless. I lean against its bulk and imagine a time when wolves coursed through a great forest, of which this wood was only a small part. I think of St. Edmund.

In the ninth century, Edmund—Saint Edmund, as he came to be called—ruled East Anglia and led his Saxon army against invading Danes. At the Battle of Thetford in 869, Edmund's Saxon army, routed, withdrew to Beodricesworth (soon to be renamed Bury St. Edmund's), where

Edmund offered himself for the lives of his men. The Danish leader tied Edmund to a tree much like this one where he was shot full of arrows. Since Edmund would not renounce his faith, he was beheaded and his head hidden to prevent proper burial. Townsfolk mourned on finding his headless body—until they heard a voice calling, "Here. Here!" Beckoned into the wood, the people discovered Edmund's head safe between the paws of a guarding wolf. After yielding the sacred head, the wolf joined the procession to Edmund's grave.

A mere five hundred years later there would be no wolves in England to guard kings, headless or otherwise.

Standing beside this tree, I think of my home in Utah's plateau wilds where, as in England, once-essential wolves neither hunt nor safeguard the land. I wonder how we arrived at this place, this time. How has it come that the snarl of ATVs replaces the howl of wolves? That the chewing of cows silences the bugling of elk? I wonder even more intently how we will get out.

Scholars and scientists worldwide tell us that functioning ecosystems provide what is needed to sustain humans into the future. We cannot mechanically recreate oxygen-giving forests or temperature-regulating oceans once their delicate complexities are destroyed. Nor can we restore animals, human or otherwise, once their unique genetics are lost. Scientists warn that even our healthiest environments are in danger. If one cared nothing for the silence of moonrise on the prairie, for the hooting of owls or the rustling of voles, if one cared for nothing but the future of humanity, then one must care for the whisper of wolves over snow. For it is only by repairing the systems that maintain us that we can regain our future. The world that sustains us is the world of the wild.

Here in England, not a mile of the wild remains. Ancient trees rise from green-lawned parks and castle estates, so rare and thoroughly known they are named, like the thousand-year-old oaks Gog and Magog standing in a sapling wood near Glastonbury's sacred sites. The only wild animals left bigger than a breadbox—the red and roe deer—pace isolated woodlots. The last wolf, it is said, was killed seven hundred years ago in Cumbria. Indeed, England may have been the first country to exterminate wolves.

Back in the United States, the wild waits, ever emptier, for our quarreling to end. It seems no warning of dire consequences, no argument scientific or practical, can relieve our medieval fear of wolves, of economic hardship, of government control. Edmund's wolf called, "Here, Here! The sacred you seek lies in the forest." What, besides the last wolf howling "too late," will motivate us to do the hard work of restoration?

~

Last week my friend Tom and I sat under Bath Abbey's ladder-climbing angels. My eyes flowed from the pews' burnished brown wood, the dust of prayers thick upon them, to the white marble wall tablets, to the ceiling's royal blue heraldic shields high overhead. In the hush and light of this soaring space my very being swelled like a hymn filling the chapel.

"Notice," Tom said, "how the pillars resemble the trunks of trees, and how, when they reach the ceiling, they fan into branches tipped with finely carved leaves." He leaned closer and whispered, "It's a sacred grove." Something inside me expanded further then, beyond the abbey walls, taking in town and hill and hedgerow-enclosed fields all the way to the open sea.

"There is no time," I said to Tom.

Below sixteenth-century Bath Abbey lie the remains of a cathedral built by the Norman king William Rufus in 1088, and below that a Benedictine abbey built originally by King Offa in the eighth century. Below that, a Saxon nunnery from the seventh century, and beneath that a Roman temple dedicated to Minerva in the fourth century. In front of the abbey and far below street level lies the original pool where, thousands of years before the Romans, Celts walked an oak-lined path to this lush spring and rejoiced in the leafy arms of a godly earth.

All around England ancient stones lean, their carvings winding and interweaving in unending Celtic knots, symbols of eternity and complexity, of life and the world. The ancient Celts, in a sacred practice thousands of years older than Christianity, acknowledged the godliness they lived within. To them the earth was the living entity from which all life sprang. The earth was not a place, but a process. To the ancient Celts, the idea of humans as stewards, as having dominion might have seemed backward. They may have said, Is not the earth our steward? How is it that we could live without the earth?

There may have been a day when ancient peoples and wolves hunted side by side in a dense coast-to-coast forest. This all changed when sheep and pigs filled our pastures, our stomachs, and the dreams of wolves. Today, the only wolves in England appear in the sanctuary of churches, where, carved in stone, they lay, a man's severed head between front paws. Nearby another man's head, wreathed in a leafy mane, watches from the wall. His eyes, clear and piercing, seem to peer not just through leaves, but somehow from within. In English churches the Green Man, a pre-Christian figure, often outnumbers images of Christ.

~

In 1848 a tree fell in Bury St. Edmund's, a tree so ancient and rare it had a name: St. Edmund's Oak. This was the tree, legend had it, to which the Danes bound Edmund. Woodsmen sent to clear the shattered tree found, within its rent heartwood, a thousand-year-old Danish arrowhead.

I walk the hill back through the manicured lawns of Dartington Hall beneath young, budding trees. Before me, oak and yew tower, seemingly ancient but nubile in their setting. A hundred years ago, gardeners planted a scene that will only reach fulfillment two hundred years from now, when these already giant trees mature. Can we do that? Can we replant the wild for a payoff we will never see? Standing in this medieval tilting yard, where lanced knights knocked each other from charging horses, I wonder what this lush, green country would look like if the religion beneath church foundations survived. Would ancient groves still shelter the howl of wolves?

Then, I understand: the religion compressed in thin soils beneath Bath Abbey survives. It sprouts in tree-shaped pillars and in light slanting through arched windows as if through wind-ruffled branches playing over the Green Man's leafy countenance. It survives in American churches where high ceilings and stained glass mimic the sacred space of forest glens. What if all those who worship below heard the light rustle of leaves over-head? In New York the Green Man watches from the walls of St. John the Divine, the largest gothic cathedral in the world. And in Utah the Green Man speaks every time I walk into the wild—a voice on the wind, in water over rocks. I pause and listen. Hikers? No, just trees talking, the grass whistling, rocks chuckling: the conversation of life. That ancient knowing survives in the watchful eyes of the Green Man and in our own. It lingers, like an arrowhead in heartwood.

Is it too late for England? I don't know. I do know that in the United States we still have a chance. But that chance is now, while wolves still howl and the wild lingers. And I know that the only real change comes from belief.

It is time to believe. It is time to believe the voices of our most respected scientists, to hear the voices of animals, to listen to the voices crying in the wilderness before the last wolf mournfully howls over the severed head of humanity between its paws. I wonder what would happen if we, like the ancient Celts, believed that our relationship with the natural world was not only practical but also reverent? What if we believed we were guarded by wolves?

Michael Engelhard

Anthropologist, freelance writer, and guide Michael Engelhard lives in Moab, Utah. He is the editor of two anthologies and author of Where the Rain Children Sleep. *Here he writes about what he learned from Alaska's Koyukon people of the "deep bonds between wolves and a human community."*

Blood Ties

There was a girl who met up with a wolf, back in Distant Time, when wolves were human. The wolf wanted her for his wife, even though he had two wives already. When he took her home, his two wives smelled her and knew she was human. After a while she had a child—a boy—and the wolf decided to kill his other two wives. He did that, but afterward the spirits of those two wolf wives killed his human wife and ate up her insides. Since then, women are never supposed to kill wolves, and they should not work with wolf hides until the animal has been dead for a while. They must follow these rules until they are too old to have children.

—Koyukon tale

My cross-country skis hiss against the surface glare, slicing mile after mile of the snowy back of beyond. Only the panting of huskies and the crunching of sled runners augment their noise. We are on our annual spring break trip, this time tracking the drifted-over road to Wonder Lake into the heart of Denali National Park. Twilight overtakes our dog team and skiers early on this brisk March day. When the cold starts to bite through thick layers of wool and down and all color drains from the land, we pull over to camp in a copse of white spruce.

After dinner in our wall tent—kept cozy by a small wood-burning stove—I step outside. By now, the ghostly, cold fire of northern lights plays overhead, fluttering in curtains of neon-green gauze. They easily blot out the scatter of stars. I stretch my sore shoulders, and my senses strain into the calm. The alleged purpose of this venture is to scout a route for a National Outdoors Leadership School course; but I really hope for a run-in with the most secretive denizen of these frozen wastes: the Alaskan gray wolf.

In all my time in the Big Dipper state, only once has a wolf graced my life with its brief presence. I was solo-kayaking the Noatak River, gliding through blanketing brush fires that pulverized tundra and shrouded silt-and-clay cutbanks. As the smoke screen lifted momentarily, I glimpsed a large canine standing still, blending in perfectly with the surrounding ashes. It appeared like a northern mirage: a creature like smoke itself. The solitary wolf on the riverbank gazed at me without curiosity or concern. He then turned and trotted away, quickly dropping from sight. I had felt strangely abandoned.

A high-pitched wailing pulls me back into the present. It wavers, rises and falls, in sync with the splendor above. It seems to come from nowhere and all places at once—piercing the night and my soul. The lone voice is soon joined by others, meshing with the pack's desire.

These must be the wolves of the East Fork of the Toklat River studied by Adolph Murie, a Minnesota wildlife biologist, between 1939 and 1941. This pioneer of wolf studies found that, like humans, packs, too, develop their own "culture," a culture that survives the death of its individuals. Thus the Toklat bunch has occupied the same dens and hunting grounds, possibly since long before World War II. It also has learned to remain largely invisible.

Our sled dogs briefly raise their heads but remain eerily silent. They curl up again—noses buried under tails—disregarding the song of their wild cousins. A breeze has picked up, ruffling the fur on my parka hood. The ruff is a strip from a wolf pelt, much coveted, since it does not frost easily when breathed upon. It is silken and rich with memories.

I attended a memorial potlatch in the Koyukon Indian settlement of Huslia years ago. The entire village had gathered in the octagonal community hall built from logs. The women wore shawls and colorful calico dresses in the traditional style, many of the men knee-high mukluks made from the leg skin of caribou. Scores of children were buzzing around the hall. After a series of speeches to honor Sophie Sam—an elder who had passed away a year before—the singing began. Groups of three to five men took turns sitting around a big-bellied drum. The rhythm they hammered out with padded drumsticks filled the enclosed space, vibrating in the pit of my stomach. Their falsetto singing was marked by fierceness, by a passion defying the finality of death. Afterward, the family of the deceased gave gifts to the crowd. They handed out beaver skins, wads of cash, rifles, blankets, beaded buckskin gloves, an assortment of household goods. I received one of many strips cut from a wolf pelt, which my mother later sewed onto the parka hood. This token embodied not only the sharing of grief, but also deep bonds between wolves and a human community.

The evening ended in a form of communion. Long tables bent under homemade casseroles, stews, bread, and muffins; "Eskimo ice cream" had been whipped into a fluff, from sugar, oil, blueberries, and pounded white-fish. Most important, though, were meat and fish taken from the land, the true foods ascertaining Athapaskan identity: moose, caribou, wild sheep, and salmon—baked, boiled, jerked, canned, or smoked. According to tradition, the elders were served first.

I had learned much about wolves from one such elder, Stephen Moses, in Allakaket, north of the Arctic Circle. When I visited for the first time, I had found his mudroom cluttered with the implements of a bush life. There were slumping hip waders, foul-weather gear, snowmobile parts, dip nets, a shotgun, beaverskin mittens dangling from a nail, and a motor saw with a chain that needed tightening. Two wolf pelts flowed from the rafters—complete with tail, legs, ears, and muzzle. Before I knocked on the inner door, I had reached out and stroked the silver-tipped fur. The gaping eyeholes and the hide's flattened appearance had left me slightly unsettled.

A dead beaver lay on the kitchen floor, half-skinned and placed on a piece of cardboard, to keep the meat clean and blood off the linoleum. Stephen invited me to sit. But before I unrolled my maps on the table, we snacked on dried caribou dipped in seal oil (a delicacy traded from coastal Eskimos). His wife Minnie meanwhile busied herself quietly with a pot of caribou-tongue soup bubbling on the stove.

The National Park Service wanted to know which areas of Kobuk River and Gates of the Arctic National Parks these hunters and gatherers had traditionally used. If they could prove prior use, the Koyukon would still be entitled to hunt there, and even to trap wolves.

Stephen pointed out the routes of his hunting and trapping expeditions. His forays had taken him way above timberline into the snowy crags of the Brooks Range and as far south as the willow-choked banks of the Yukon River. In the mountains and plains to the north, bands of seminomadic Koyukon had hunted Dall sheep and caribous for thousands of years, in friendly competition with packs of wolves. The meanders he drew on my maps, with felt pens of various colors, resembled the tangle of wolf wan-derings and territories wildlife biologists chart on their maps. Stephen's eyes took on a distant expression, as if he were reliving each mile on the trail. His crinkled, leathery face relaxed.

"That *teekkona,* he keeps caribou strong." An ecological understanding at least equaling that of western science found expression in these few words. A lifetime observing the animals under natural conditions had made this man a wolf expert and better hunter. I sensed admiration for the sleek and efficient predators under his words. With a callused finger, the elder tapped on their den sites, and those of bears, black and brown. He said that the quality of pelts—fox, mink, marten, lynx, otter, beaver, wolverine, and wolf—was best in January and February, when temperatures plummeted and the animals grew coats dense and shiny. Though he was too old now to go on long trips, Stephen remembered how to intercept wolves near their kills, which bait to use and how to set and disguise traps. "They are smart, just like us," he chuckled.

In soft, lilting, village English laced with Koyukon expressions, he recalled a rare black wolf he had caught more than four decades ago. He had traded its pelt together with other furs in Kotzebue, at the Bering Strait coast, for his first decent gun. Wolf pelts are still valued highly. They can bring $450 or more at the fur exchange in Fairbanks or Anchorage, cash that is needed for outboard motors, rifles, four-wheelers, and snowmobiles.

Stephen spoke at great length about respect. He told me about the web of taboos surrounding this animal, an animal whose spiritual power is rivaled only by that of wolverine and bear. I had read in an early ethnographic account that in pre-mission days, Athapaskan hunters honored a killed wolf like a chief. They carried it to camp on their shoulders. Then they brought it inside the hunter's home, propped it up as if alive, and a shaman would set a potlatch-style banquet before it, to which the entire village contributed. When the wolf guest had eaten its fill, the men took their share.

When I mentioned practices and beliefs I had come across in my research, Stephen became serious. He nodded, in recognition of an age-old kinship.

Currently passing on his knowledge to a grandson, he stressed the rules that guide contact with wolves. A rifle used to shoot one should always be left in the front of the house, and for four days afterward. To appease the departed spirit, a chunk of dried fish should be put into the dead wolf's mouth, or a choice piece of caribou backstrap burned as an offering. "If you don't do this," he concluded, "he will turn on you." Disregard of the rules of conduct will unfailingly bring bad luck, injury, disease, or even death, to the hunter or his family.

According to another Distant Time tale, the pact binding Koyukon and wolves is ancient: Long ago, when such things were still possible, a wolf-man lived among humans. He shared their lives, participating in their hunts. When he left the people to return to his own, he promised that wolves would sometimes leave kills for them. They would drive caribou toward human hunters, in exchange for favors received while they were still human. And thus, to this day, Koyukon men who come upon a fresh wolf kill are entitled to take what they need.

These days my old down parka is stored away in a box. Its wolf ruff has turned a bit ratty. I no longer live in Alaska, but in a state where the last wolf was killed more than sixty years ago. In my new home state, a debate rages about the reintroduction of wolves. Brother Wolf is ensnared, once again, in the agendas of game managers, ranchers, hunters, politicians, and environmentalists.

Winter nights in the Wasatch Mountains can be crisp and clear and studded with stars, like up north. But they are devoid of the serenading of wolves. No longer can tan-and-gray mists be glimpsed from the corners of your eyes. No new stories take shape, renewing blood ties between them and us. Like grizzlies, wolves have been banned from their native range. The price of a few cows and sheep—or even deer—seems small compared to the loss pervading these forests.

There is reason to hope, though.

On November 27, 2002, a black male wolf was trapped near Ogden, Utah. Tracks of a mate were found nearby. The radio-collared animal turned out to be a stray from a Yellowstone pack two hundred miles north, seeking to expand its territory. After an absence of nearly a lifetime, wildness had returned.

At times I feel tempted to relocate to Alaska, to a place where the voice of the forest can be heard in the night. I still stay put, believing that, like the Koyukon, we can learn to live with *teekkona*.

Becoming Wolf

The pieces in this section explore various ways of thinking about ourselves as kin to wolves. We share the animal body, these writers say, though we often forget or deny it, and we may also share something of the same wild spirit. And so if we open ourselves up to their particular wisdom, wolves can help us return to ourselves, our full, true selves, as they teach—or remind—us how to live richly in the wild world.

Charles Bergman

Charles Bergman teaches at Pacific Lutheran University. His articles about wildlife, especially endangered species, have been widely published in magazines like Smithsonian, National Geographic, Natural History, *and* Audubon; *his latest book is* Red Delta: Fighting for Life at the End of the Colorado River. *This essay considers many ways of thinking about wolves, including King Lear's lesson about all that we share with these animals and Bergman's own midnight dance to the howl of a wolf in Alaska.*

Life Like This Wolf

In the final scene of *King Lear,* the distraught king enters with his dead daughter Cordelia in his arms. His first words are not words. He howls. "Howl, howl, howl!"

The same Lear who earlier in the play was so afraid of becoming an animal has become wolf. He is not *like* a wolf. He speaks *as* a wolf. Howling in unspeakable pain, Lear slides dazed into the animal, becoming wolf.

Lear's howl is the culmination in the play of an almost obsessive interest in the ways in which humans become animals. On the heath, during the storm, Lear finds himself "comrade to the owl and wolf," living like a "belly-pinch'd wolf." Poor Gloucester, eyes gouged out, can no longer see to find his way. He must "smell his way to Dover," living like a dog. Lear and Gloucester are a brace of canines.

Edgar assumes the disguise of the madman and the beggar, Poor Tom. He speaks of himself as "Brought near to beast." On the heath, Lear says Tom is "the thing itself," "a poor, bare, fork'd animal."

I remember once hearing a biologist say that the most important thing to know about a wolf is that, for people, it is always a symbol. It is the image of the devil preying upon Christ's sheep. It is a seducer preying upon young girls. It is a criminal, an outlaw in the West stealing ranchers' cattle. It has even become a terrorist in President Bush's recent campaign ad.

But the wolf is not a metaphor. The question of the wolf—like the question of Lear's howl or Gloucester's sense of smell—is not what it is *like*. The question of the wolf is what it *is*. Listen carefully to Lear's howling wolf. It's the best wolf in literature, because it actually has "speaking" lines. What does it say? It says "no" to human meaning. It says "no" to representation.

Maybe it is possible to feel the wolf from the inside, as Lear did. If you want to find out what howling like a wolf does to you, you've got to try it.

I teach a course on writing about animals, and one of the best things we do is visit a place dedicated to wolves: Wolf Haven, in Tenino, Washington, not far from where I teach. For a couple of decades now, it has been a home and sanctuary for captive-bred wolves—wolves that were born as pets, or in zoos, but are no longer wanted. Wolf Haven takes them in.

As we learn when I take my students there, most of the wolves we see will live out the rest of their long lives at Wolf Haven. They live in chain-link enclosures, which feel different from most walled-in zoos. Less separates us from them.

Each of the animals has a name. Each has a biography. These are particular wolves. Onyx, for example, is an old male, born on April Fool's Day, 1987. He's described as "affectionate." It quickly becomes obvious for most of the students, this is their first encounter with real wolves. We get close to them. Sometimes they even come up close to investigate us, sticking their noses through the fence.

The best part of the experience for me comes at the end. We are invited to howl with the wolves. If we begin to howl, the wolves usually howl too. The students are always incredulous. They look at me, and look at each other, embarrassed and reluctant. Occasionally a student will howl. Usually, they won't.

What they do is watch me. And smile. I don't care. I howl. The sound comes from deep in my throat, and it's a miserable imitation of a wolf howl. I do it long and let it waver, drawing it out. The wolves are very forgiving. Usually one howls back. When one does, a whole furry chorus of them gets going. You can hear the individual voices, each with its own howling style.

We are a chorus of creatures. As I howl with these captive wolves, the chain-link fences dissolve. We join each other in our voices, and I might as well be one of the pack.

I'm best when I'm stupid, and to get stupid you have to turn off your brain. The intensity of the experience loosens me up and opens me out.

King Lear is itself a play concerned with the Renaissance debate about animals. Are humans animals, or something better? What is it to be human?

The humanists were arguing that humans could be anything their minds wanted them to be—including angels and gods. Such views were flattering to human pride, but it was bad news for the rest of the animal creation. For humans to be better, the other animals had to be repressed. Not just the animal in the world, but the animal inside the human as well. The animal became the emblem of the stupid, mindless other—all that the human is not.

The human is, ironically, the only animal that defines itself as the animal that it is not. Paradoxically, the animal is always invoked in defining the human: we are not beasts. The animal is necessary to say who we are yet is forgotten and rendered invisible in the instant that it is invoked. We need the animals to be human, and we render them no thanks, and considerable scorn, in the bargain.

Shortly after Shakespeare, in the seventeenth century, the humanists' way of thinking about the animal won out—thanks mainly to Rene Descartes, who was aggressively anti-animal. In the four centuries since *King Lear,* the gap between human and animal has widened.

Yet in *King Lear,* Shakespeare is doubtful. Lear gains a greater dignity in the play, but it is not a transcendent dignity. It is a dignity that is shared with other creatures, located in Lear's howl. It is the dignity inherent in all living, and suffering, creatures—man and beast alike.

Perhaps more than any other animal, *Canis lupus* embodies the battle between persecution and recovery. The effort to reintroduce wolves throughout the country is the external, conservation dimension of the struggle to recover the repressed animal inside the human. It is not clear still whether persecution or recovery will win out. Or perhaps it's more accurate to say, that we seem strangely uncertain about what it means to "recover" wolves in the country. How many, for example, is "enough" wolves?

No other animal that I know of evokes such intensity of feeling, for and against. It is the intensity of this passion that attracts me to wolves. They have helped me find myself, howling me back to myself.

I have sought them—or rather followed them—around the world. I have seen white wolves in the high arctic of Ellesmere Island, ghosts against the snow. I have caught glimpses of dark wolves in the wet woods of Vancouver Island. I have watched wolves in single file move through the deep snow of a Minnesota winter and heard them howl on Isle Royale in Lake Michigan. I've seen two Iberian wolves trotting home to their den on an unforgettable morning in the mountains of Asturias, Spain. I've held the pup of a red wolf. I've been in the enclosures of captive Mexican wolves near Mexico City, as Mexican biologists plan for the reintroduction of the remnant creatures in the north along the boundary with the United States. I've crawled into the den of a wolf in Alaska and looked into the eyes of the wolf pups in a pile. They growled at me, and I felt I had come as close as I would ever come to pure wildness.

Of all my experiences with wolves, the one that has entered most deeply into me came when I camped on a bluff in the mountains of the Alaska Range. A biologist and I were dropped off by helicopter at a very remote site. We set up camp overlooking a gravel bar on a river below. Just off the river, we knew that wolves had a den site. From the bluff, we could watch the wolves in their comings and goings. They would come out of the forest and into the open on the gravel bar.

Since it was late June in Alaska, it never quite got dark at night. The sun would disappear behind the mountain peaks, but from 2 A.M. until 4 A.M., it was twilight—evening and dawn all at once. We slept with our sleeping bags beside the campfire and under the protection of an enormous cedar.

In the pink half-light of an arctic night, I woke up one night to the howl of a wolf. I lay there in my bag and listened. The fire was still burning beside me. I realized the wolf was on the gravel bar below. I shot from my bag and looked down. The alpha female stepped out into the open beside the river. She was easily recognizable, this very particular wolf, by her distinctive white coat with a gray saddle across her haunches. She moved like an apparition in the thick light.

I watched her pad across the bar toward our bluff. She stopped, lifted her snout, and raised another cry. It was like a moan, rising and falling in pitch, trailing off in a haunting, heart-piercing, mournful note. The eerie howl rolled off the surrounding peaks and came at me from every side.

At the den in the woods, the pups heard their mom, and answered. Their howls were even higher pitched, a yapping chorus.

I let myself go in a moment of happy surrender that I still do not really understand. I did not howl back—did not want to scare the wolves. Instead, I danced on the bluff to the wolf's howl, trying to feel this wild wolf. Hoping to grow a tail. Dancing to save myself.

Pam Houston

Pam Houston's books include the short-story collection Cowboys Are My Weakness *and the novel* Sighthound. *When she is not working as Director of Creative Writing at the University of California–Davis, she lives near Creede, Colorado. Here she tells the story of a long day of muddy driving through a landscape of coexistence and some kind of communication, or recognition, among species.*

Opening Day on the Denali Highway

The year was 1987, and it was the first time I had ever been to Alaska. The fiction writer I was dating had been invited to the Midnight Sun Writers Conference in Fairbanks, and I had gratefully tagged along. It was the middle of May. I remember sitting on the front deck of the Chena Pump House watching an orange sun edge sideways toward the horizon. It was one in the morning, and the guy I was talking to, the husband of one of the U of A poets, I think, offered me the use of his truck the next morning. "It'd be a shame to spend all your time in Fairbanks." he said. "This way you can get out a little, see a bit of the country."

I'm pretty sure that he did not mean by that, "Please take my truck tomorrow and cover as much ground as you possibly can in a twenty-four-hour period," but seeing Alaska had been a dream of mine since I was old enough to pronounce its syllables. I picked up the late model half-ton Ford at seven the next morning and got out of town as fast as I could.

Alaska's highway system, such as it is, is concentrated in the southeastern part of the state, an almost equilateral triangle that connects Anchorage with Fairbanks, Fairbanks with Tok, and Tok with Anchorage on the Parks Highway, the Richardson Highway, and the Glenn Highway, respectively. Bisecting that triangle is the Denali Highway, a 110-mile graded dirt road that goes from Cantwell, Alaska, near the entrance of Denali Park, east (away from the park and the peak) to Paxson, on the Richardson Highway.

Snow closes the Denali Highway in early fall, and for more than nine months this huge section of wild lands on the south edge of the Alaska Range is the exclusive domain of the animals.

Too many years have gone by now for me to remember who it was that told me the Denali Highway was opening for the summer that very May morning. The guy at the gas station where I filled up before I left Fairbanks? A voice on the radio? The waitress at the diner where I stopped for sourdough pancakes with wild Alaskan blueberries? Whoever it was also told me that there would still be twenty-foot snow banks on either side of the road, and that it would be "a muddy bitch" up there for certain. They also told me that if I attempted the journey, I would see more wildlife than if I were at Lion Country Safari, that the plows had been working up there for upwards of three weeks, and that the animals come right in behind the plows and start using the road like their very own highway until June, when the tourists begin to arrive.

I did pause for a moment to think about how I would feel if I had loaned my truck to a stranger who was thus presented with the same moral dilemma I was facing. I paused for another moment to make sure I knew how to get the truck into four wheel low. Then I drove the 115 miles to Cantwell and turned east past the barricades that only that morning had been pushed to the side. I wasn't on the road five minutes when I encountered my first wild animal, a moose, contentedly chewing on some broken willow branches that the plow's blade had exposed. He raised his eyes at me as I chugged past him, more in interest than alarm, and never stopped chewing. The mud was deep in that first section, sometimes up to the axles, but the Ford crawled along determinedly—it was used to Alaska, I reassured myself repeatedly, even if I was not.

As we climbed higher in elevation, the meltwater had collected and formed huge puddles between the roadside snow banks, and the truck crashed through the thin layer of ice on the surface into jaw-rattling ruts below. To the north, the peaks of the Alaska Range were starting to shed their swath of cloud cover as the sun climbed higher, and I made a guess at which ones were Deborah, Hess, and Hayes, the three highest peaks in that part of the range. I saw a trumpeter swan swimming in a roadside lake, stopped the truck on the most sold patch of mud I could find, and got out to take photographs. I walked to the edge of the water and had the swan all lined up in my viewfinder when I heard a tremendous beating of wings behind me. I turned just in time to see her mate coming in for a landing, flaps down, scrawny legs extended, honking like crazy and aiming straight for the back of my head. I hit the ground face first. The swan landed in the water just in front of me, then turned and made a couple of false charges in my direction as I backed toward the truck, clicking the shutter all the way. I was dismayed to find that in the short time I was out of the truck it had sunk about halfway to the running boards. The truck spewed tremendous plumes of mud getting out of there, but it was only a moment before we were climbing again between the towering banks of snow.

To list the animals I got up close and personal with that day feels a little bit like bragging: a wolverine; a porcupine; a flock of ptarmigan (recently turned to their brown summer plumage, but still wearing their white après-ski boots); a small herd of Dall ewes and lambs, and later an aged ram; an interior grizz, jogging along in front of the truck for nearly a mile, his cinnamon tips glinting in the afternoon sun; something like two hundred caribou.

When I first saw the wolf, I mistook it for a German shepherd. I was near enough to Paxson by that time that it seemed possible it was somebody's pet. His coat was almost true black, thick, healthy, and as shiny as a show dog's, but when I saw the glint of his gold eyes, I knew he didn't belong to anyone but himself. The black wolf was coming up the road toward me. It was late in the day, and I had just been starting to feel a little guilty about where I had taken the nice man's truck, about how many hours I had been gone from Fairbanks, about how the truck was so covered in mud you could no longer tell what color it was.

I let the truck glide to a halt (I hadn't gone more than fifteen miles an hour since leaving Cantwell), and the wolf, too, slowed from his trot to a standstill. I was thinking about reaching for my camera, realizing I'd never get the picture between the streaks and smudges and hunks of mud on the windshield, when the wolf lifted one paw, as if in greeting. I thought immediately of my favorite Ed Abbey essay, in which an Arizona mountain lion makes a similar gesture, and Ed realizes he is not quite brave enough to shake the lion's hand. I dropped my camera back onto the seat and eased the upper half of my body out of the window, so the wolf and I could be face to face.

"You are the most beautiful thing I have seen all day," I told the wolf, "and today, that is saying a great deal."

The wolf licked his lips, put his paw back down on the roadway, and looked at me thoughtfully. He was so much a dog and so much more than a dog. He was a dog raised to the nth power.

The wolf stretched once, in classic downward dog position, turned to face the snow bank, and without even one step of a running start leapt up and over its twelve-foot top. I jumped out of the truck and climbed on the muddy hood. If I stood on tiptoe on the top of the cab I could see over the snow bank, see his black tail waving as he nimble footed it over the sun-packed snow. I watched until I couldn't tell the difference between his form and the line of willow tops he was following.

The half-ton Ford and I splattered back on to the pavement near Paxson at ten that night. There was still plenty of sunshine, but I was pretty sure the chances of coming across an open car wash would be slim to none. I still had 164 miles to cover to get the truck home to its more-generous-than-he-knew owner. Imagine my surprise when, 154 miles later, I came around the corner into the town of North Pole, and there was a car wash with an inflatable Santa on the roof, open twenty-four hours.

A few years later, I had begun to make part of my yearly living guiding Dall sheep hunters and backpackers on the northern slope of these very same mountains. The bush pilot would drop us off and inevitably say something like, "I'm not going to come back and pick you up unless you bring me a wolf carcass or two for my trouble." When he did, I would remember the glint in that black wolf's eyes and realize it was that look, more than any other thing I saw that blessed day in May, that insisted I return again and again to Alaska. It was always tempting to take the pilot's bait and start shrieking, but I'd ultimately hold my tongue. I'm not an Alaskan, after all. I'm a Coloradoan, living in a place where soon, I hope, I'll be seeing wolves close to home. If I am really lucky, I'll be given another chance to shake hands.

George Sibley

George Sibley lives in the valley of the Upper Gunnison River and teaches journalism and regional studies at Western State College of Colorado. His new collection of essays is Dragons in Paradise. *Thinking about Wolf 293F and the border collie who lived with him for many years, he contemplates what wolves might teach us if only we could learn to listen.*

Never Cry 293F

I was moved—meaning shifted a little off my usual base—by a newspaper story late in June 2004: a dead wolf had been found beside Interstate 70 here in western Colorado. A she-wolf with a radio collar.

Since the wolf had a radio collar, it was no real problem to find out a lot more about her. She was known to those who had installed the collar as No. 293F, a two-year-old member of the Swan Lake Pack in the northwest corner of Yellowstone National Park. She had last been "seen" there (electronically, I assume) in mid-January 2004, and had presumably headed south in the spring in search of a mate with whom to start a pack of her own. Instead, her road-crossing luck ran out at the really big road—after how many smaller roads?—and she encountered a car or a truck that broke her back and left her to an ignoble and probably painful death.

Months later, this story still flits and skulks along the margins of my mind. It comes to me at odd moments, like when I am listening with professional sympathy to a student here at the college telling his tale of woe about why this or that isn't done yet, or when I'm sitting in a department meeting about what to do about whatever it is the legislature is doing now in the name of god instead of taking care of state business, or when I'm with the group dithering about the possible advent of a Wal-Mart Supercenter here on the downslopes of the Elk Mountains (otherwise prime wolf terrain). Into these odd moments this she-wolf lopes, in the eye of my mind: now moving along in the open under an evening moon in a place where movement is easy and safe, now slipping along the edges of woods and high weeds where movement is less safe but still easy, now standing beside the mystery of a road trying to figure out the strange alien life there.

I've thought quite a bit about the "wolf reintroduction" program in the contiguous United States, but mostly in that way—my mind slipping out of whatever it's supposed to be thinking about, into thinking about wolves.

Sometimes I think this: What's our problem? Or, what's this the solution to? Or, is wolf reintroduction part of a solution or part of a problem? Or more generally, is noblesse oblige part of a solution or part of a problem?

And other times I think this: If I were a wolf, would I want to be "reintroduced" into the forty-eight contiguous United States? Should we have figured out how to ask them first, if they wanted to be reintroduced? The history of Western civilization is full of episodes of Euro-Americans moving bewildered peoples around from one place to another without asking their opinion (Bosque Redondo), or just moving in on them (Iraq), always for what has been determined to be their own good or improvement, or ours, or (we always sincerely imagine or hope) both. I find myself wondering how this wolf thing is different from all that.

But other times I just think of it the way wolf 293F lopes into my mind—no "real" memory because I have never really seen or even heard a wolf. But I've seen them, or even been with them or something like them, in the old memory that wakes up in dreams. Like the dream a long time ago, the same year I got kicked out of the Army. In that dream, I was running along just below a ridge under a frozen moon, and I was some proto-mammal from before we mammals had subdivided into things like wolves, lions, humans, foxes, and hedgehogs. I remember very little of that dream except for what I can only describe as a sense, both calm and awake, of being where I belonged, doing what I was made to be doing—an unusual feeling then, or now for that matter.

And since I doubt this was or is my dream alone, and since what humans do (Americans anyway) is to strive to "realize our dreams," it figures that we would have to invest some of the wealth we're borrowing from the future into the Reintroduction of the Wolf, to bring that dream—our collective "old memory"—into what passes for American reality. Trying to bring a bit of our own old wildness back—but in a radio-controlled way.

Given all that—I obviously don't know exactly what to think about wolf reintroduction. But I do find myself hanging a slender hope on it—an almost embarrassingly strange hope. My hope involves the radio collars. And memories of a border collie that graced my life for a time.

~

Border collies are—and are intentionally kept so by their breeders—a little closer to the proto-mammal ancestor of all canid species than are most other breeds of dogs. While most dogs get bred and overbred for all kinds of specific human purposes, from rat riddance to neighbor intimidation to identity reinforcement, border collies still live pretty close to the original "social contract" between some wolfish animal and some human that was probably somewhat wolfish, too.

This was a contract set up around the idea that collaboration might be better than contention and competition: the wolf and the man would work together to protect the sheep from whatever (mostly other packs of wolves and other bands of humans) in exchange for a sharing-out of the meat rather than fighting over it. No doubt the real wolves thought the contracting wolves were total sellouts—just as some of the real men probably thought that the contracting humans were inviting the devil into their midst.

But it worked out in many cases, and continues to work out. We got our border collie from a friend who raises them, and works with them. I've watched him work both sheep and cows with the collies, and watching that collaboration gives me hope that life on earth might eventually amount to something really interesting and positive.

What I remember most about the border collie who lived with us for a while—fourteen years—was the sense of an intelligence that was (I eventually realized) somehow beyond me. The capacity for abstract reasoning is supposed to be something that is unique to humans, but I saw that dog figure out things that involved thinking through them—from finding hidden things, to figuring out the connection between going over the fence and spending the next day or so on the chain. And she had a vocabulary of quite a few of our words. My partner, for example, who usually wakes up after I do, could send the border collie downstairs to tell me it was time for a cup of coffee. Easy stuff for the dog; to really see them think, go up to the September dog trials in Meeker.

For several years after becoming aware of her intelligence, I displayed a typical human arrogance about it. I would say to visitors, "behold the limits of intelligence when it has no opposable thumb, no vocal cords." And she would just sit there looking at me when I would say that kind of thing, looking at me with those unfathomable eyes, probably saying in her way, "You poor dumb shit." And eventually it occurred to me that the failure of communication there wasn't her inability to speak to me; it was my inability to hear her. She was able to receive messages in my language to a rudimentary degree, but I never got that far with her language (although I did come to understand simple eye messages like "out" or "time to eat").

It began to occur to me that the development of vocal cords, and a resulting dependence on vocal communication (and its literate extensions), might have been a limiting rather than an expansive progression.

~

We know enough about wolves to know that, like border collies, they convey a lot of messages without having to make noises. Humans who have lived together for a long time can also do that to some degree—and a very few of us are good at picking up unspoken messages from others we don't even know that well. This "gift" is probably a genetic hangover from when we were more broadly in touch with things around us, although it doesn't seem to be a major selection factor in a civilized society.

But the radio collar intrigues me, and provides that slender thread of hope. As I see it now, we have quite a number of wolves—hundreds even—running around the Rockies with radio collars on their necks transmitting signals into the world around them. When we have the funding, we intercept these signals and plot them on maps and graphs. In our more astute moments, we attempt to overlay these maps on other maps we have created of the landscape and its coverings, and then we interpret and analyze and write scientific papers.

But my hope—a somewhat ridiculous hope, but those are the only serious hopes—is that somehow the wolves, consciously or unconsciously, will start adapting their capacity for intuitive communication to their radio frequencies, and will start broadcasting something that will help us know—well, help us know something we need to know but so clearly don't. Yes, it is a long shot, but let's face it: our electronic extensions may be more sensitive than our natural ones these days, and we certainly spend more time and money transcribing and interpreting digital signals than we do anything else. If there were something coming through the wolf's collar, actually from the wolf, we might find it electronically where we no longer can empathetically.

The wolf formerly known as 293F, for example—because of her radio collar, we probably knew more, in a certain kind of way, about her, her ancestry, her travels and her fate than she herself knew, at least in the kind of way that we know things—but that is just the kind of knowledge we think we want from the wolves. On the other hand, what kind of knowledge do we need? Well, I'd be interested to know: what were her hopes, what were her fears, as she tried to figure out Interstate 70? What was her relationship with the universe as she tried to launch her own Wolf Reintroduction Project for the geopolitical real estate development we call Colorado?

But that is still pretty anthropocentric knowledge. It'd be more useful, maybe, to know what she thought as she ran down and killed a rabbit or a sick deer on her way south. Or, most important—what she thought when she left the Swan Lake pack, her family, her world. Was she asked or told to leave because the pack had outsized its territory? Do wolves actually have a sense of what they need to do to keep things in balance—even, or especially, to the extent of keeping themselves in balance? And even if they know that kind of thing—what were the feelings of the rest of the pack as they watched her leave, however necessary they knew it was? They are mammals like us; they don't just know things, they feel.

And why would I say we need that kind of knowledge from wolves? Because it is so clear that we are far, far out of touch with any balanced relationship with the universe, and maybe wolves are better at that than we are. Why else would we be inviting back fellow large predators that we'd earlier killed off, if not for some kind of consultation?

Such a consultation, of course, would require that we stop talking long enough to really, seriously, listen, which is probably what most makes it a ridiculous hope.

∼

The fact is (tragedies like that of 293F notwithstanding), the reintroduced wolves are doing pretty well. Today, from thirty-one wolves planted in Yellowstone National Park a decade ago, there are maybe 750 wolves ranging out into the Rocky Mountain region. As far south as Interstate 70, for dead certain. And though we aren't yet communicating directly, we have learned some useful things from them.

Wildlife managers tell us that the elk herds in Yellowstone are healthier for the presence of the wolves—the herds are thinned down, made leaner and quicker through the presence of large predators that are happy with the low-hanging fruit, never mind the trophies. And tied to this, the land is apparently becoming healthier, too—aspen are growing again where the elk had nibbled them to death, beavers are returning and making ponds among the aspen, songbirds are returning to roost in the trees. All because the wolf is back shaping up, thinning down the elk herd.

So the essence of my hope, I guess, is that the reintroduction here of large predators outfitted with transmitting one-way neck radios will lead us eventually to a true "rewilding" of our own awareness, a more courageous confrontation with our own natural reality—specifically, that there is no herd on earth more in need of thinning down, shaping up, returning to health, than the swarming human herd.

As I write this, for example, winter is coming on and the media are full of lamentation and whining about an absence of flu vaccine. Our president suggested that the healthy and strong forego the vaccine, leaving it for the weak and infirm and vulnerable. Otherwise some of them might die—thereby thinning down the herd a little. How about just forgetting about flu vaccine entirely, and letting a little natural thinning happen?

It is difficult to talk about this without feeling like—and undoubtedly being perceived as—some kind of an insensitive and inhuman monster. You may want to assault me, if only with questions: Are you prepared to die for the good of the herd? Would you condemn your own grandmother to death by flu? Actually, I had a grandmother who, at ninety-something, wanted to die so badly that she had to be heroically rescued by a nurse when she tried to go over her seventh-floor balcony. She was saved, and enabled to spend the last years of her life in a nursing home that she hated until finally a review of her diminished financial assets indicated that she should not be pulled back from a case of pneumonia.

How would wolves respond to this "flu vaccine emergency"? The whole situation would probably perplex them. A species swarming so badly that it can only collect the excesses in urban sinks where, increasingly, the only serious governance involves crowd movement and control—and the species is dithering about how to keep its weak and infirm alive? With many insisting that even unwanted children must be brought into the world against a parent's wishes? And making it illegal for the old and tired to leave on their own accord when they are tired of living, to make room for the young? If we could pick up on what the wolves are transmitting, we would probably hear the sound of incredulous laughing.

But I think (trying to think like a wolf) it would be a mistake to believe that the health of the herd requires a mean-spirited "toughness" from us. I think it would be a mistake, for example, to accept the cultural indifference we are beginning to show toward the spread of AIDS, famine, genocide in Africa as a "healthy attitude." Or to see as "natural enough" the young predators spreading through the impoverished world, the young boys and girls growing up with dead eyes and assault weapons, kids who have never known anything but the advanced psychoses of a species going mad and sick from its own excesses.

I think (trying to think like a wolf) what redeems a wolfish acceptance of death from brute indifference may be the wolfish capacity for singing like a wolf. As I said, I have never heard the wolves sing, but I lived for a while in a neighborhood with a pack of fourteen sled dogs, long-legged beasts that were probably even closer to the wolf than my border collie was. Two times a night, I would half-wake into their song leader's low note, then the others coming in with their notes, and for maybe half a minute, half awake, I would be simply overwhelmed by their song of the terrible sad beauty of life on earth, sung as only those courageous enough to face its terror and beauty can sing it.

So, one hopes: as we fiddle with radio collars and computer maps while we burn down the world around us, as we shuffle ever closer to the ever worse cultural and natural disasters that are growing out of the excesses we lack the wolfish will to begin addressing—one hopes the wolves will continue to improve the health of the herds, and will continue to grow in numbers themselves, perhaps beyond our remote control. And eventually, if we won't do it ourselves, then they will, in the poet's words, "lope into the lighted city" and start doing here what we won't to improve the health of the herd.

The reintroduction of large predators may be, as much as anything, a prayer for salvation from ourselves and our lack of both the natural will to do what needs to be done and the natural grace to sing the sadness of having to do it.

William Pitt Root

William Pitt Root shares his home in southwestern Colorado with two wolf-dogs, one of whom, Lulu, is the happy protagonist of this poem commemorating both the pleasures and challenges of such a domestic arrangement. He is the author of many books of poetry, the first five of which are gathered in Trace Elements from a Recurring Kingdom.

To the Wolf at My Door: A Sort of Apology

While I type
     in she trots
          out of open daylight,

a hundred pounds of girl wolf,
     her laser-gaze golden,
          her soft ears half cocked.

When I lean down
     to rub muzzles with her,
          sandgrains on her chin

give her away:
     She's been
          in the garden again,

devotedly burying bones
     or digging them up,
          and now she's smuggled

into the study
     with all its musty books
          the stuff of fields and forests,

the odor of
  earth freshly stirred,
    in a word

fertile ground!
  Bless you,
    Lulu Garou,

you've done the work
  cut out for you.
    Now let me do mine.

Michele Murray

Michele Murray lives on the brink of South Park, Colorado, and writes about the outdoor life for the Mountain Gazette *and other magazines, newspapers, and websites. Here she recounts her transformation from city-girl bassoonist to "River Rodeo Girl" to nature writer—and describes all she learned from her wolf-hybrid, Banjo.*

Lurking with Wolves

I love to lurk in the wilderness. I learned to lurk from a fuzzy-butt, four-legged companion—a wolf-dog named Banjo. I miss her. And when I think on the events with Banjo that led me to the places I now lurk, I commonly wonder at how precarious fate and fortune can be: a little dip in one direction and *poof!* you're a bassoonist in New York City; a little dip in the other direction and *poof!* you're a naturalist writer in the mountains of Colorado. I've found that in matters significant to personal growth, fate and fortune may accept a little nudge here and there—the kind of nudge that might bring a bassoonist out of New York City, through the Grand Canyon, and on to participate in the matter of wolf reintroduction in Colorado. All the nudge needed for this transformation was simply to lurk in the woods with my wolf-dog and face my fears.

I have lots of them. I fear the topic of wolf reintroduction because I hate controversy. I truly am stunted intellectually. I dread getting involved in "grown-up" things. I even willed my breasts not to grow. I so dreaded adolescence and was such a devoted tomboy that I died when I was forced to wear a bra. I felt like a cat on a leash. I willed my tiny boobies to stay small and stopped wearing bras as soon as I heard that women were burning them. (Thank God for the women's liberation movement!) I wasn't making a statement by going natural—I was simply trying to stop biological processes from happening in my alien body. I wasn't hip at all. I was a bassoonist. I didn't smoke or drink or have a boyfriend. As my childhood passed, I practiced the bassoon all the time with no interest in the world outside of my reeds. And when I was twenty-one, I moved to New York City to play in the symphony.

Fate and fortune would have me, a professional bassoonist, accept an invitation to hike and float the Grand Canyon with a group of geologists. I bought a sleeping bag, backpack, and harmonica in a store on the Upper West Side, bid temporary farewell to my bassoon, and caught a cab to start the journey.

The trip started in Bryce and Zion National Parks and culminated in the Grand Canyon with a two-day hike down from the rim to arrive at the brink of the Colorado River, where a crew of dory guides stood waiting beside their vessels looking awfully intense. It was the famous Martin Litton Company's last run. That should be enough said about the quality of the trip—the emotional content for the guides, the lasting forever of our galaxy's touch on our unsleeping eyes. We were unified with the river, the canyons, the sun, the sand, mudslides, rain, and beer.

I was a bassoonist riding the rapids with my knees hanging over the bow! I clung to the bowline with one hand waving in the air above my head and rocked onto my back when huge waves crashed against the hull. I became River Rodeo Girl! The guide was delighted to have a young woman's crotch adorn his bow. (Was I a young woman? Or a tomboy still, after all these years?) I played the harmonica until the river took it from me, my audience applauding when the instrument made a "ker-plop" into the water. We slept in sand divots. We cooked dinner for the guides. We hunted for caches of beer hidden in the canyon walls, stashed there by clever river guides who did not want to portage the excess out and up on trips with teetotalers. We smashed the empty coffee cans crammed full of the day's debris and carried our poop out in ammo cans.

Everything they say about the Grand Canyon is true, but no one has mentioned the thunder of silence—a sound vacuum in your ears that makes you think you are hearing outer space with the planet of Venus ringing light waves into your head. No one mentions naked sand games or laughing yourself to sleep. Nothing has been written about the aperture of the canyon's mouth outlining our universe, as can been seen lying flat on your back using all of your peripheral vision with wide eyes. I returned to the city, transformed. I mailed most of my belongings to my parents' home and gave the rest away. I moved to the river at State Bridge Lodge, in Colorado. I still fear writing about the Grand Canyon. I fear not being able to capture its essence.

Fate and fortune brought a box of wolf-hybrid pups to State Bridge Lodge. I met Banjo, my life's best friend. I raised her with trepidation about the instincts she was born with. I wondered if she would have the potential to kill or maim another dog—or worse, a child. I had no idea what to expect of her.

I hated wolf-hybrids before I got to know Banjo—rather I hated the idea that some apartment-dwelling ski kid who just moved to the mountains thought having a wolf-hybrid would be cool. My veterinarian warned me not to tell people she was part wolf. I trained her in an almost militaristic discipline to follow my hand signals and to resist impulsive behaviors. (She was attuned to body language—hand signals were her preferred method of communication, and eye expressions, and if I had had ears that could move and a tail, she would have liked those too.) She did not bark. She did not chase. She was my constant companion, even attending my classes at the university, where I began to pursue a master's degree in geology.

I continued to live at State Bridge Lodge and commuted to my classes in Boulder, 150 miles away, by stacking classes into three days a week. Banjo and I lived in my Toyota hatchback. We camped in the woods outside of Boulder and on the banks of the Colorado River at State Bridge. Banjo and I hiked every day—whether it was on the streets of the city through throngs of pedestrians and other dogs, or on a deer trail through cedar and pinyon following and tracking bobcats, elk, mule deer, rabbits.

I learned from Banjo to move from tree to tree and to stand perfectly still, only moving my eyes to look for animals. I learned how to move amongst the animals without disturbing them. I learned to sit and observe and to wait for the herd to graze through. If we were to disturb (or chase) animals every time we saw them, then the elk and deer would move off to find a more secure place to live.

In this way, Banjo and I tracked and learned the ways of the local wildlife. We watched mule deer make a bed and go to sleep on top of each other in a pile. We were overtaken by a herd of elk with their calves and had to stand with our backs to a tree as a maddened cow elk pawed the ground into a mess at our feet with her anger over our presence (but she let us go). A bald eagle dangled in a jet stream just out of arm's reach to get a good look at us crouching in a sage patch. We spooked a napping cougar off a ledge above us to leap over our heads in its escape, and I just about had a heart attack.

Fate and fortune brought cellular changes to my wolf-dog. In her ninth year, she died of cancer. She had been to more mines and national parks than most geologists. She had traveled to three countries. She caught a trout, rode in a canoe, windsurfed, and went sailing. She had flown in a jet and a hot air balloon. She even rode in a limousine in Denver. And she never bit anything other than a sandwich (a very mean sandwich). She wore hats, too.

It was for Banjo's sake that I decided to participate in the matter of wolf reintroduction. I commenced research, conducted interviews, drank whiskey, and, despite my fear of controversial issues, focused an opinion. Sort of. At the least, I compiled a list of fears relative to being killed by wolves:

1. Car accident getting to the wilderness.
2. Heart attack or other biological malfunction.
3. Being struck by lightning on a ridge.
4. Drowning in a river accident.
5. Getting shot by a trigger-happy hunter, rancher, cop, or drug dealer.
6. Bleeding from an open wound (because Coloradans might chew their arm off if trapped under a boulder).
7. Sunstroke (been there).
8. Hypothermia (done that).
9. Dehydration (*Giardia*-induced).
10. Breaking through ice over a lake or river.
11. Being caught in a catastrophic event (flash flood, tornado, wildfire, avalanche, mudslide, or volcanic debris flow).
12. Fatal fall from a great height (not a barstool—higher than that).
13. Complications due to gangrene (from falling off a stone wall with one's pants around one's ankles while mooning the Amtrak train and subsequently breaking one's leg in twenty or so pieces—no person in particular in mind).
14. Fatal asthma induced by allergic reaction to external stimuli (insect, plant, food).
15. Skin cancer.
16. Victim of mistaken identity with some other bad woman in a mountain bar.
17. Rabies from someone's cat.
18. Snapped neck or cranial fracture in horseback riding/dirt bike/motorcycle/ATV accident.
19. Microbial infection: bubonic plague from sleeping in rat-infested trapper's cabin; virus from touching a wild rabbit.
20. Kidney or liver failure due to drinking every liquid in sight (sometimes with gangrened friends or pistol-bearing fools).

21. Mine or cave collapse.
22. Electrocution (I once saw a Boy Scout tent covered in downed wires in a blizzard).
23. Suffocation (I never play in abandoned refrigerators any more).
24. Being gored by a buffalo, stomped by an elk, dragged off by a bear, or pounced on by a cougar.

and last . . .

25. Being stalked and eviscerated by a pack of wild wolves.

I miss Banjo, as I would miss a very dear, once-in-a-lifetime friend. She was the best person to spend my life with. We will have our ashes mixed, when the time comes, and spread into the Colorado River at State Bridge Lodge. It's in my will. I am grateful to be able to share such love across the bounds of a different species.

There is fate and fortune lurking in the woods, and in the matter of wolf reintroduction, they may need a little nudge. I give you this: an opportunity should be made available—an open window, a significant gesture, some kind of impetus—to return a wolf to the wild for people to see. Who knows? Some bassoonist may be so moved by seeing a wild wolf that she may grow up to become a naturalist writer.

Antler

Antler, the Poet Laureate of Milwaukee, Wisconsin, is the author of Factory, Last Words, Selected Poems, *and the forthcoming* Ever-Expanding Wilderness. *He occasionally teaches at Naropa University in Boulder. This poem expands on the ancient story of a child raised by wolves to imagine a boy raised by everything that's wild.*

Feral

Boy raised by wolves, boy raised by panthers,
       boy raised by dolphins, boy raised by sequoias,
Boy raised by spirits of plant-eating dinosaurs,
       boy raised by the cave behind the waterfall,
Boy raised by clouds, boy raised by snowflakes
       every snowflake different,
Boy raised by rainbows, boy raised by stars
       that existed before this Universe
       in Universes that existed before this one,
Boy raised by a crystal embedded in bedrock
       one mile below where you stand
       or one hundred miles below
       where you stand,
Boy reared by an anaconda in the jungle
       that became his teacher and best friend,
Boy raised by eagles, boy raised by fireflies,
       boy raised by luna moths, boy raised by pussywillows,
Owls, gorillas—boys raised by them,
Bears, otters—boys raised by them,
Bigfoot, Loch Ness monster—boys raised by them,
Boy raised by geodes, boy raised by aurora,
       boy raised by marijuana, boy brought up by mushrooms,

Boy nurtured by a huge field of fresh fallen snow
        with no footprints in it in moonlight,
Boy raised by whales he never sees
        whose minds a mile down in the Pacific Ocean
        control his every move,
Boy suckled by volcanoes,
Boy raised by hurricanes and earthquakes,
        tornado-raised boys,
        boy raised by echoes from seashells,
Boy raised by undiscovered pyramid on the Moon,
Boy raised by reflection of Mount Everest
        upside down in a dewdrop,
Boy raised by being able to tell
        what kind of tree
                by smelling its bark in the dark.

Dona Luongo Stein

Dona Luongo Stein, the host of the Poetry Show *on KRFC in Fort Collins, is a former Wallace Stegner Fellow at Stanford University. Her newest book is* Entering the Labyrinth. *Highlighting the links our culture often sees between wolves and human sexuality (consider the phrases "wolf whistle" and "lone wolf"), "Lady" imagines an intimate encounter of a "pure form."*

Lady and the Wolf

I am in my ladyskin coming down the stairs,
My thigh level, perpendicular
To the wall. At the door

You are in your wolfskin,
Your amber eyes glow, your pelage
Bristles above your tie.

Your round ears are luminous
From the moonlight. Coming
Down the hall, I hear a hum,

A singing motion of silk.
Your long legs approach,
Move slowly under their fur.

Behind me on your toes
You prance, then your webbed feet spread
As your nails click on my floor.

I feel you pant toward my neck
And before we reach a proper door
I hear a knife sharp zip—

My ladyskin's on the floor.
Did you unbutton your wolfskin
So we stand staring
At what pure forms our souls are in?

Laurie Wagner Buyer

Laurie Wagner Buyer lives in Woodland Park, Colorado. She writes and publishes poetry, fiction, and nonfiction; her Spring's Edge *won the Beryl Markham Award for creative nonfiction. Here she tells of her changing relationships with the idea of wolves—as a "city girl converted to the religion of the wild," as a rancher's wife, and as the recipient of a mystical apparition—and, along the way, a matching series of relationships with men.*

Where There Are Wolves

Wolves and men have always come to me in odd ways, strange places, and weird times.

The first was a portrait of a wolf painstakingly carved onto a polished elk antler rosette, the words "dweller of the silences" along with the artist's initials and date, 1974, carved on the back. It was that artist, who called himself Makwi Witco, Crazy Wolf, that I came west for in 1975, taking a train from the outskirts of Chicago to Whitefish, Montana, then working my way to a tiny triangle of land that the locals called Moose City. Nestled between Colts Creek and the Northfork of the Flathead River, the cluster of old homestead buildings became my home for three and a half years. A quarter-mile north, the Canadian border cut a swathe through old-growth timber. Glacier National Park lay east across the river. Flathead National Forest stretched for miles south and west with only little enclaves of private property reserved for summer homes and a few hardy year-round residents. A wilderness stronghold, the spot harbored every major predator and prey species of the North American continent including deer, elk, moose, mountain lions, grizzlies, black bear, and, the artist insisted, wolves. Though the last documented sighting of a wolf had been long decades gone, the artist turned mountain man had heard the eerie howl far off in winter distances and had followed tracks much too large to be a coyote's in remote locations too inaccessible to be anyone's wandering husky or malamute. Makwi Witco lived for the chance to see a wolf in the wild.

When word reached him that a rancher downriver had shot, then buried a wolf, he was furious, but also pleased that his assertion that there were wolves in northern Montana was accurate. Rumormongers altered the story immediately, saying the rancher stated only that some big stray dog had been chasing his stock and he put an end to it. Who would confess to shooting an endangered species when the act carried a huge fine as penalty?

While I shared the belief that isolated individuals or an occasional mated pair traveled the place we called home, I was more drawn to wolves in the mystical-mythic sense: the lone wanderer, the master predator evoking fear and wonder, the devoted mate. I ached for landscapes wild enough to support wolf populations, just as I ached for landscapes that would embrace humans dedicated to wilderness. I was a city girl converted to the religion of the wild, the politics of preservation.

More fawn than ferocious hunter, drawn to the gentle ways of deer and elk, I felt most at home in the company of goats and horses, but the wolf was there, a shadowy presence I could not ignore. One fall, when the artist packed horseback into the high country, I woke from a sound sleep on the downstairs sofa with every hair standing rigid with anticipation. Some sound coming out of perfect silence had wakened me. I strained my ears to hear. The wood stove sighed and crackled. The hound moved to the door and whined. Out in the barn, goats' bells tinkled. Then, again, wavering notes so high on the melodic scale they were barely audible. Not the crazy-chorus yodel of coyotes. Since I'd never heard it before, I couldn't be certain, but guessed it was the howl of a wolf. When we left the Northfork of the Flathead in June 1978 in search of wilder country, wildlife biologist Diane Boyd took up residence in the old homestead cabin on the river. With scientific documentation, the wolves we always knew were there became a reality.

Makwi Witco and I didn't find a wilder place to roam as a mated pair. A breech in our vision sent me back to college, and sent him north into Canada where, like the wolves he loved, he wouldn't have to come into contact with human beings. I lost touch with the man, but the wolf shadowed me. I read Barry Lopez's *Of Wolves and Men*. I wrote to Diane Boyd. I corresponded with Rick Bass about the Nine Mile wolves. In subtle ways, the myths and legends and real life stories of wolves continued to find me. I wanted wolves to survive. I wanted them to reclaim old territories. But I felt opposed to man's mucking around with the wolves' intrinsic nature. Knowing they were being tranquilized, captured, tagged, radio-collared, and made into the subjects of scientific study sickened me. While

I understood that wolves needed the help of man if they were to thrive, my pained heart said, "Just leave them alone to live their own lives in their own ways."

Then, I went to work for, fell in love with, and married a fourth-generation cattle rancher who was known by family and friends as a lone wolf, a solitary recluse who preferred the snowed-in isolation of his high country home to town. My environmentalist-preservationist attitude came smack up against the reality of a life lived close to the bone, to a livelihood dependent on keeping predators at bay to prevent stock losses. My husband, whose family had come West by covered wagon in 1879, argued with me about wild horses, coyotes, beaver, bear, and lions. It didn't take long for me to become educated. Pulling beaver dams day after day, seeing land overgrazed not by cattle but by burgeoning herds of elk, chasing a bear who chewed into the grain box, seeing a birthing heifer with her hind end eaten out by coyotes, gave me a whole different take on man and his interaction with wildlife.

On this Wyoming ranch, competition for land, grass, water, and space was fierce. Idealism versus reality—what we wanted versus what we got. It was one thing for me to argue for the right of all wild things to live and have their place in the natural world; it was another to face the fact that the loss of one calf meant no groceries for a ranch family for a month. It became an argument not of right or wrong, but of who ate and who didn't. Though wolves hadn't been seen in the Wind River Mountains in anyone's recent memory, the possible threat of wolf predation on livestock remained.

Feeling like a bit of a turncoat, I found myself debating the fine points with environmentalist friends: Was there a difference between saying, "Well, it's only one calf, what does it matter" and "Well, it's only a wolf, what does it matter?" What mattered to each human being involved was the thing they worked hard to nurture and to save. What mattered was what affected each individual's daily life, which issue manifested itself in the heart. Lucky for me, my husband and I only had to contend with coyotes bothering newborn calves on occasion, but just a few years after we left the Upper Green River in Wyoming for Colorado, the first grizzlies and wolves drifted south out of Yellowstone Park. Predation on the Green River Drift, on ranches around Pinedale and Big Piney, and on the wintering elk feed grounds became documented facts.

Wolfless Colorado became my home in 1988. My husband returned to his family's original homestead roots in South Park outside of the small town of Fairplay, and I followed. With each move in my life, I drifted farther and farther away from wilderness haunts and dishearteningly closer to cities. Not a choice I preferred, but one necessary for survival. The wolf went where there was prey (whether rabbits, deer, elk, cattle, sheep, or horses). People went where they could make a living. My husband and I worked his cattle ranch on the South Fork of the South Platte River for fifteen years and managed to preserve the land in perpetuity with a Colorado Open Lands conservation easement. While we saved the ranch for his children and grandchildren, we were unable to save our twenty-year relationship. The irony of everything became the essence of what drove us apart: a subtle but deeply ingrained difference between choosing domesticity and wanting to run wild.

These days, a somewhat disgruntled town dweller, I walk on asphalt dodging cars, bikes, people, and dogs. The chance of seeing a wolf in the small mountain town where I live is nil. Yet, the wolf remains part of my psyche, part of my consciousness, part of my intrinsic desire. I don't read newspapers or magazines. I don't watch the news. I don't take part in any organized movements for the environment or for animals, or even for people. Instead, I go to wild places when I have an opportunity. I sit and listen, take time to be quiet and respectful. I pray for all things, including the wolf, and I pray for our Earth. It isn't much: one voice whispering in the wilderness. Yet I believe that if everyone would take time, if each person would pray, our world would change. We'd find a way to coinhabit the Earth with wolves and with each other. We'd find the balance that means, among many things, "an aesthetically pleasing integration of elements."

Where there are wolves in wild landscapes, the balance of nature between predator and prey is more stable, more whole. Where there are people in wild landscapes, the balance of nature is most often disrupted and disturbed. And yet, the human soul needs wildness in order to know and understand itself at the most primal level. If there are answers to the questions we ask ourselves about wild places, about wolves, about human interaction or intervention, then those answers are found in the wolves' howl, the wind's song, the river's symphony, the eagle's scream, the fragile flower's intricate pattern, the stars' magnificent design. How many centuries of looking and listening, observing and absorbing, will it take before we finally figure it out?

I last encountered a wolf in May 2004 in the Guadalupe Mountains of Texas. It was a short exchange of energy that occurred on the final morning of a six-day backpacking sojourn during which we'd seen perhaps a half-dozen people while traversing remote, rugged terrain. Somewhere between Mescalero and Pine Top, I dropped my pack to make a pit stop. I waved "go on" to my new mate, Carlos, who had the cyberspace name containing the phrase "alpha wolf."

During my moment of maple-shaded reverie, the hours and days of near silence I'd just experienced settled over me, a sweet continuum of memories I knew I'd hold close after my return to town life. Savoring a patch of early sun, I stood motionless, letting a slight breeze dry the sweat from my back before I hoisted my pack.

After miles of climbing rock to rock on uphill and downhill slants, I found the stretch of trail before me easy on the feet and eyes. Mostly level, the narrow, well-worn dirt trace meandered through thick stands of spruce and pine, in places its outline cushioned by the dry duff of fallen needles. Walking through dappled sun and shadow, my face lifted to the shifting light, I closed my eyes and moved forward guided by hearing and the sensation of what my feet could feel.

I raised my eyelids and spotted Carlos' black and red pack drifting through the trees ahead of me. The trail curved back on itself, then yawned into a straight stretch. Increasing my pace to catch up, I found a comfortable stride and once again closed my eyes, savoring the far off whoosh of wind in treetops, scattered bird song, squirrel chatter, and lizard skitter.

Something prickled my skin. I slowed, but did not stop, then opened my eyes with care. Carlos hiked fifty feet ahead of me, his pack swaying to the long reach of his legs. Then, a gray wolf crossed the trail between us, coming out of nowhere, disappearing into nothing. I slammed to a stop. Blinking. Breath jammed in my throat, knees quivering. What had I seen? Wolf, my heart sang. Impossible, my intellect countered. I sucked in a huge breath, exhaled a giant sigh and closed my eyes. Again, like the rerun of a film clip, the wolf trotted out of treed shadow into the sunlit frame of the trail, head low, eyes riveted straight ahead, tail level. Looking neither left nor right, he disappeared without sound, nose first, then shoulder, ribs, haunch, and tip of dark tail, into a void.

I opened my eyes. Carlos stopped and turned, stared at me.

"What?" he mouthed.

I swallowed, then whispered, "Were there ever wolves here?"

"Sure. Why?"

If I told him, would he think I was crazy, delusional, hyperexhausted, or dehydrated? Taking a chance, I explained the experience. "Was it a vision?" I asked.

"Maybe," he said. "It has happened to me here. Could be the little people having fun with you. Or Apache spirits sending you a guide."

"Come on," he said when I did not move. "We've still got a long way to go to get off this mountain before dark."

I stared at the spot on the trail where the wolf had walked. What if it was some kind of a time warp where I could fall in and disappear, too? I stepped forward, arms out for balance, breath held, gooseflesh rising, sweat breaking out on my palms and under my arms, the sharp scent of my own primeval musk filling the air.

Disappointed that I had not vanished into an earlier time, or shape-shifted into a she-wolf, I looked back at the place where the wolf had been. I searched for a track, a scratch mark, the dark glimmer of fresh urine, anything to show me that what I'd seen was real. Tears needled my eyelids as I remembered the seasons I had lived on the banks of a Montana river, when I had lived where wolves lived. Perhaps with enough prayer, the night would come again when I'd be wakened by a wavering chorus of nomadic howls.

David Ray

*Recipient of the 2001 Nuclear Age Peace Foundation Award,
David Ray lives in Tucson, Arizona. His newest book is* The
Death of Sardanapalus and Other Poems of the Iraq Wars.
*In this startling poem, David Ray thinks about wolves, Freud, and
a young woman he once saw in India—and how they suggest the
contrast between the innocence still found in animals and some
other cultures and our own culture's shame about our own natural
bodies.*

In Praise of Fecalcentrism

The study of wolves is, we are told, fecalcentric,
for their scat tells a great deal about their DNA
and whether they gorge on acorns or rabbits
and perhaps whether a pup chases his tail in circles.

As children we too were innocent and our scat
was golden, but we were soon shamed into disgust,
as if the lower body were to be feared. Thus, for Freud
the study of humanity was also fecalcentric

as he tracked in his journals his own dreams about
"little heaps of excrement of all sizes and degrees
of freshness," nor did he leave out analysis of "a long
stream of urine that rinses everything clean so that

the patches of excrement come off easily and fall
into the opening." The great man's feelings aroused
by such dreams "were the most pleasant and gratifying."
They made him think of the Augean stables cleansed

by Hercules, and himself as Hercules. "The stream
of urine that washes everything clean is an unmistakable
allusion to greatness." The wolf, of course, marks
his vast territory with a golden stream that gilds all lilies.

In more innocent countries than ours one sees humanity
not yet shamed into renouncing what has passed through
their bodies. What in my life was ever more beautiful
than the girl whose upraised hands like those of a caryatid

held a basket laden with a gleaming globe of fresh dung
like a high chignon, and under it her smile so glorious
that had I been a wolf I would have followed her home?

John Nichols

John Nichols is best known for his novels like The Milagro
Beanfield War *and* The Voice of the Butterfly. *His environmental
essays include* If Mountains Die, On the Mesa, *and* The Sky's
the Limit. *He has lived for thirty-five years in Taos, New Mexico.
Here he describes his regular expeditions into the wild places near
his home where he can be free of the "stain" of human activities
and instead answer the strengthening call of the wild.*

High and Alone

During the last few years I have climbed regularly through the mountains
near my home in Taos, New Mexico. I have managed to hike almost twice
a week across terrain that lies between eleven thousand and thirteen thousand feet. From late October until May or June, I have done my adventuring on snowshoes. Spring, summertime, autumn . . . all seasons are marvelous in alpine country. I have rarely met another human being in the
places I escaped to, a major attraction of my journeys.

There aren't trails through the land of tall cliffs, wide boulderfields, and
talus slopes that rise steep and imposing. Until autumn snows become deep
and unstable I've trudged onto the highest mountaintops and ridgelines
where I can overlook dozens of other peaks, ravines, and wide, mysterious
basins. My companions are pikas and marmots, sparrow hawks, and ravens
soaring on the thermals. Bighorn sheep graze the exposed ridgelines year
round, even during the most savage storms of winter.

I am slowly memorizing the plants and flowers, the bugs, birds and animals of the area. Often, over winter months, my snowshoes make the only
tracks through several feet of white powder. I have plodded around a bit-
terly cold and frozen place where the only movement besides myself was
an occasional Canada jay, or an eagle overhead, or clods of dislodged snow
falling with explosive bursts through the branches of Engelmann spruce
trees.

I am an aging man, now sixty-four, who works very hard to attain that wild universe. I love being alone in the natural world, without another person around, and with almost no evidence of human activity prescribing the landscape. I try hard not to piss or shit up there because I prefer not to make animals anxious with my human stain. I perch quietly atop boulders observing several square miles that I have to myself.

There are often snowstorms or rainstorms or fierce winds to battle. Occasionally, excessive heat or rockslides or snow avalanches scare me. The vastness can be intimidating. But my solitary presence above the forest usually makes me euphoric. I am close to nature on its own terms, uncorrupted by people's activities: biology in the raw.

One day last July I sat on a hillside surrounded by cornlilies and larkspur shoots at twelve thousand feet. I peered through a spotting scope across the basin at a band of young bighorn rams butting heads and humping each other in a snowfield on the flank of a tall mountain. The bighorns are threatened animals who only a decade ago were reintroduced to the wilderness area bordering my hometown. They have thrived on that small island of rocks and tundra above the spruce and fir trees. I watch the sheep, fascinated by their behavior, learning their habits, amazed at their survival. They are spectacularly adapted to the harsh terrain. Little lambs bounce down almost sheer cliffs. During the rut, big rams clobber each other and then freeze, holding the pose, silly and strangely heroic.

It's rare to experience nature relatively unscathed by *Homo sapiens*. I come and go quickly and have little impact on my surroundings. Despite the hard work, I always feel at home and at peace above timberline. When I say "at peace" I don't mean an obsequious placidity of the soul in soporific repose. I am aware that rockslides might crush me, I could break an ankle among the boulders, lightning will strike from building clouds, hypothermia or heatstroke may catch me by surprise. I understand that some plants, like cornlilies or death camas, could poison me. It it's June or July there will be a bear and two cubs inhabiting the marshes I've traveled through—I must take care not to offend them. A constant "danger" makes me alert and tuned to my environment. I carry no cell phone, I tell nobody where I am. If I screw up, no ambulance or helicopter will come to bail me out.

So when I say "at peace" I mean simply that I am wide awake, I feel that I understand the place and its rules. This creates a sense of balance in proportion to my environment that I almost never feel when I am down below fighting the human rat race in a befouled habitat where everything (and everyone) seems askew.

True, I'm only a visitor to the high country. Yet physically, psychologically, emotionally, I believe I am relearning my relationship to the natural world that created me. This is exciting, it gives me joy and hope, and I think humility also, because my experiences take place where that natural world dominates and I am small indeed.

Those moments, with that responsibility and awareness of my surroundings, are a trifle nerve-wracking but very precious. I shed a lot of my human abstractions there. I pick up coyote turds and bear scat, sniffing them curiously. I am thrilled by weasel tracks across the snow. Ravens chatter around me, and I squawk back at them. Their acrobatic flying is sensational.

By paying so much attention to the plants, the animals, the weather, I'm training myself for "survival." The more I learn the more precious natural life becomes. I feel a powerful connection with stones, clouds, and willow bushes, letting free the animal inside that truly describes my humanity. If there is to be a human future, shouldn't we all relearn exactly how we are connected to the biology that sustains us? And admit that we need wolves to complete the picture?

At sixty-four, with an infirm heart and other medical conditions, I expect that I am also preparing for my death by caring deeply for the organic miracle from which we evolved. When you feel merged with the cycles of seasons and weather and bear cubs growing older, you lose the fears generated by humanity's specious heavens and hells, property obsessions, Botox injections. Frankly, I couldn't care less anymore. Nature is the foundation of life and death, and I belong to nature truly.

Tomorrow, I will snowshoe up to a lake that is starting to thaw. I'll search for ravens, bighorn sheep, the first brown creepers of spring. Maybe I will see a red squirrel, a ferruginous hawk, or the tracks of a pine marten. There should be Clark's nutcrackers, chickadees, gray jays, and juncos. I'll have to start early, when snows are frozen, because later on I could sink up to my crotch in the slushy stuff. The weather report predicts blue skies and an unseasonably warm afternoon—

But I hope that enormous clouds arrive, and that they are filled with thunder and lightning . . . and the distant howl of a resurgent predator.

Kent Nelson

Kent Nelson is the author of the novel Land That Moves, Land That Stands Still, *which won the 2004 Colorado Book Award. He has run the Imogene Pass Run three times and the Pikes Peak Marathon twice. Describing one long solitary run through the high San Juans, Nelson imagines wolves returned to this prime habitat; "I run to train," he says, "but they run to live."*

Running with Wolves

The country around Ouray is daunting—cliffs and dark timber and steep everywhere you look. Ouray is 7,700 feet. To the south are Mount Abrams, 12,800 feet, and Hayden Peak, 13,248. To the west are Whitehouse Peak, 13,700, and Mt. Sneffels, 14,150. East is the Amphitheater, a cirque that gets the evening sun and sometimes, in summer, shows a pink or lilac alpenglow. North is downhill, where the Uncompahgre River flows. It's great country for bear and elk. Great country for wolves.

This mid-August morning I am doing my last long run before the Imogene Pass Race to Telluride (eighteen miles, 5,400 feet elevation gain) coming up the first Saturday in September. My plan is to run from my house in Ouray up the Million Dollar Highway to the Bear Creek Trail, up the trail to the Yellowjacket Mine, up to the left and across the tundra on American Flats, then to connect with the Horsethief Trail, run down and up and down and up again to the Bridge of Heaven. My daughter is to meet me at the Bridge with water and replenishment, or maybe to carry my body home.

At fifty-four, I should know better than to try to run twenty-five miles over such terrain, but I'm in the best shape of my life. I started running the mountains the year before, did the Los Angeles Marathon in February, and have kept running. I run alone.

I start at 6:30 A.M., because if I need rescue there will still be light. I carry two bottles of water in my fists—I'm used to this—no pack, no rain gear. I have on a long-sleeved shirt over a short-sleeved one, because it's cool in the shadows. The first part on pavement is uphill to the trailhead, not too bad, but the trail itself is steep. I puff up switchbacks for a thousand feet, then turn the corner onto the miners' trail along the gorge, a straight-down drop to the creek. I've hiked this trail a dozen times, and every time I'm petrified, but running it's not so bad because there's no time to think of falling. You watch the slate fragments, the rocks, the roots. It's steady uphill to the meadows.

The meadows are where the high country opens up and the world starts. Cliffs, aspens, deep grass, and, higher up, spruce and fir. On the open hillside a herd of elk graze—cows and calves, a couple of spike bulls. They're far enough away not to spook when I run past.

Wolves would get along in this country. Elk are plentiful. Deer. It's more rugged terrain than the Lamar Valley in Yellowstone, where the wolves have been reintroduced with success. This area gets pressure from hunting, but it's a big space. The only big predators are coyotes and bears and mountain lions.

Another mile farther I pass the Yellowjacket Mine at 11,160 feet. Slowly. I'm tired after two hours' running uphill, and when the trees peter out, I walk the trail along the rushing creek, heading north toward American Flats. Over an intermediate rise I encounter two bighorn rams lying on the scree. They get up but aren't threatened. I'm above the trees, and all around are patches of grass, arnica and mallow, rivulets of snowmelt. The water is music.

I'm aware of fatigue. The brilliant pale blue of forget-me-nots is too bright, the Parry's primrose pulses fuchsia, the marsh marigolds are incredibly white. I drink the end of my second bottle of water, fill it from cold snowmelt, and put in an iodine tablet.

At 10:30, I crest out of the high valley at 12,580 feet onto American Flats and run again. The alpine tundra stretches a mile in every direction—gentle swales, rocky outcrops, green. A coyote lopes along and disappears over into Cow Creek. Across a wide ravine a half mile away I see animals—pale gray, and I'm aware they're sheep—not bighorns that belong here, but domestic sheep grazing on the national forest. They trample the tundra and eat too much grass, leaving the land vulnerable. They pollute the creeks and spread diseases among the native bighorns. It's everyone's land, but the government does some people favors.

I find the trail marker for Horsethief and bear left into Difficulty Creek. Four hours. Still running. The narrow trail descends similar territory, but off the Flats it's wilder, less used by human beings. I'm staggering a little now, but still okay, though I have to descend a thousand feet and climb another thousand to Bridge of Heaven. I smell the unmistakable rancid hot musk of elk. The odor is so vivid that only minutes ago they must have been where I now am.

Then I imagine wolves. They are up in the dark timber on the other side of the gully, *Canis lupus,* looking not at me, but at the elk that have gone around the nose of the ridge. The wolves make signs to one another, circle, looking anxiously toward the Alpha, who's still deciding whether it's the moment to run. The struggle starts again. Predator and prey. A balance of animal and natural habitat. A ripple of fear runs through me, too, for I'm not excepted from the sway of instinct.

The trail curls into the gully and up along the slope where the wolves are. I can't see them now, but I know they're there. I'm in the moment. A howl goes up, and I'm inside the howl, running up the flank of the hill. It's a long grade, insistent and brutal, especially now. I'm tired, but I don't stop. The wolves are loping easily above me through the trees. They stretch their legs, tails down, mouths open to sweat. No aches or pains. I run to train, but they run to live.

As I weaken, they gain strength. Ahead, the trail disappears to the left, and as I come around the curve, I imagine the wolves will be there waiting. But the valley opens again, scoured by an old avalanche, a sunny ravine of downed timber, grasses, and flowers. No wolves.

I have seen wolves in Alaska—a black wolf running away on the tundra on the North Slope, a pack on the Denali Highway, one lone wolf of Nome—and, in Yellowstone, a dozen wolves gathering on the hillside near a herd of elk. That could happen here.

Coming out the ridge I see the elk, maybe twenty of them, climbing the far side of the ravine. They go straight uphill, heavy animals that tire easily. But there is nothing for them now to fear.

I stop for a moment and in between heavy breaths drink some water. The sun slides behind some clouds, and in the shadow is a chilly breeze that makes me shiver. I see where the trail goes—into the basin and then up along Difficulty Creek and back again into the trees. It's a long climb up from where I am to the Bridge of Heaven, where my daughter had better be waiting. I cap the water bottle and close my fist around it and start running again, imagining wolves.

Todd Simmons

Todd Simmons lives in Fort Collins, where he edits and publishes the semiannual literary/art journal Matter. *He is currently working on a series of novellas concerning stillness and movement. Here he thinks about how the wolf's nomadic motion can inform our own activism. "Like me," he writes, "wolves are moving toward a world they want to live in."*

Hello, Nomad

I have never seen a wolf.

~

In the spring of 2002, with a homemade yurt strapped to my failing Ford Escort, I left Idaho. I remember the sentence I had written in my journal a few months before that prompted this uprooting: *Build a yurt and wile my days away walking circles and reading poetry.* Though I live for wildness—one of the reasons I originally moved to Idaho—I fled that mountainous state with its grizzly bears, wolverines, mountain lions, and wolves. While racing through the mountains, devouring myself in some sort of quarter-life crisis, I was savage as any wolf, running rampant toward that which would sustain me, nomadic as hell, caring little for boundaries.

I should tell you about the life I left: about working for the National Park Service, based at the University of Idaho, in some sort of rock-'n'-roll park ranger position—jet-setting about the country, bouncing from park to park, hotel after motel, meeting after meeting. My job, my life, my trajectory—everything added up, the long hours spent in school were finally paying off. Everything worked. But what I saw every day at our nation's "crown jewels" disturbed me. I would watch people get out of their cars, attend to their coolers and cell phones and sunscreen, and not see the land the same way I was seeing it.

We humans have the uncanny knack of missing things that are clearly in front of us. It's like this: multicolored, plastic real-estate flags closely resemble Buddhist prayer flags. Seen from a distance, you could mistake one for the other: someone who didn't know better might think they represent similar things. Some breeds of dogs—say, malamutes, or even German shepherds at a distance, running through dark woods—closely resemble wolves. But a wolf is no more a malamute than a real-estate flag is a Buddhist prayer flag. At our national parks I saw wildness paved over and subdued: the land saturated with signs pointing where to look. To see out of my solipsism, and outside of the stagnant management practices concerned mostly with moving people as quickly through the parks as possible and telling them where to look, I had to move.

~

Shortly after leaving Idaho, I stopped fleeing and devouring myself long enough to look around. I found a place for the yurt in the mountainous outskirts of Fort Collins, Colorado. I walked circles around a book I wanted to write. I read poetry for a while. After a time I figured out what I wanted to do with my brief flash of life. Then I really began to move.

I started a literary/art journal called *Matter* and involved myself with a community of people desiring change in the world. I embraced activism and moved like mad organizing and taking part in poetry readings, war protests, critical-mass bicycle rides, recycling and composting programs, publishing essays and poems and stories about the change I needed to see. I planted a garden and built a bathhouse on the side of the yurt. The itch to move on, to be nomadic, morphed into something else, and now I'm still moving relentlessly in and around Fort Collins. I find my movement sometimes frantic and wild—there is never enough time, and never enough sunlight—but there is an endless amount of work to be done in our communities to bring about a saner—and by that I do mean a wilder—world into existence.

As I was digging in my heels here in Fort Collins, another creature seemed to have followed me down from Idaho—a wolf! Here in Colorado, right now, wolves are showing up, in newspaper editorials and in the flesh, trying with all the life they have to move back into this state. Like me, wolves are moving toward a world they want to live in. Who can guess what it is in their blood that makes them move? Wolves are coming back, and we may even help them back ourselves, and I want to see one running past the yurt. It will scare the hell out of me, but I want to see one—I need to see one—if only to fan the fire under my ass to work even harder toward a world I want to live in.

～

A wolf lunges and goes after a kill; a wolf goes full tilt, a wolf is moving wildness—no romantic notion, no pretty poem left on the pillow after the love is gone. To me, wolves represent the world saying plainly and simply: "Enough of this civil and serene, calculated and sedentary; here's some wildness—so let's have some damn movement." I need this wildness, I need its rhythmic, edifying jolt to my solipsism. I am reminded of what Robert Motherwell said: "The main thing is not to be dead." I hear stories of wolves, and talk about wolves with my friends, and run circles around the yurt hollering hot damn wildness!—wolves, here in Colorado!—and then get back to work in the garden to turn up the beets.

I get all frothy-mouthed, wild-eyed, hair-raising-on-the-back-of-my-neck excited when I think about wolves in Colorado. I get all tanked up on hope and optimism and inarticulate passion. But then I remember how we've treated wolves in the past and wonder how it will be different this time. Do we have problems with wolves not because they are so different from us in their bloodthirsty, wild, and nomadic ways, but because we echo them, and they us, continuously? Wolves kill each other, as do some humans. Wolves love the taste of flesh, as do some humans. Wolves move and desire and live wildly, as do some humans. We're all experimenting daily on how to survive anyway, so what are worried about? Are we worried about the wolf being wrong for us, as it takes some of our cows and pays little attention to our most sacred cows—our laws and borders and notions—or are we worried about looking at the wolf in ourselves?

Wolves, keeping true to their blood, will keep moving. Depending on our lifestyles and our use of our laws, guns, traps, poisons, good intentions and management plans, the wolves will establish themselves in this state, or they won't. My greatest fear is that they will move off the Earth—will lose the will to live, or have it stolen from them—and move off into the spirit world, or, if you are not so mystically inclined, simply into the world of history books and art and campfire stories.

～

Living too close to half a dozen honeybee hives has made the yurt a favorite place for bears to visit in the springtime. I lay awake one night in the yurt a year ago and heard a great crunching and smacking and sighing. If that is a bear, I thought, that is a bear that does not desire to be disturbed.

In the morning the beehives were destroyed, and some bear was asleep somewhere, covered in honey. Skunks thought that the space underneath the yurt's floor was their domain, and I tried in vain for six months to convince them otherwise. When I least expected it, they moved on. Spiders found dozens of places to live, and I couldn't keep up with the killing, so they do as they wish. For a few weeks each spring, wasps appropriate the Plexiglas dome at the top of the yurt and then move on when I least expect it.

Life in the yurt makes me wonder why we spend so much energy trying to banish part of this great community we are forever moving with. Now that wolves are coming back, what will we do this time as they gather around us? Will we deflect their movement with hatred and vengeance? Will we continue killing them? Continue stripping the world of its wildness? Continue paving ourselves out of existence?

Wolves are moving quickly, their thick footpads pounding pavement and meadow and forest floor, moving in the same world we are, great blurs of fur and fang. Should we reintroduce the wolf? I say bring them back yesterday, and bring them back in droves. I want to see a wolf, so I'm keeping my eyes on the horizon, and moving like a son of a bitch all the while.

Landscapes with Wolves

In this final section of Comeback Wolves, *writers consider both the practicalities and the subjective possibilities of restoration. They write of recent reintroduction projects in New Mexico and Arizona and of the efforts to return wolves to Colorado. And they anticipate a future not so far away when we will again live in a world with wolves, thanks to the hard but ultimately rewarding work of hope, hands-on actions, persistence, imagination, and storytelling.*

Gregory McNamee'

Gregory McNamee likes to think that the only way he survived living with a red wolf for several years at his home in Tucson, Arizona, is that he had read one or two more books about canid psychology than the wolf had. Author of In the Presence of Wolves *and* Blue Mountains Far Away, *among many other books on animals and landscapes, he tells here of some of his experiences following the first stages of Mexican gray wolf reintroduction in the Arizona highlands. "The Blue Range is only a start," he writes. "We have a world to win."*

On the Hunt

The old man wipes his brow and gazes into the desert light. It is early April, there is dust in the air even at this early morning hour, and his eyes are moist, rheumy with age and the grit on the wind.

"I heard a wolf once," he says. "I was a boy, living up at my grandparents' place up on Eagle Creek. Least I think it was a wolf. That's what my grandpa told me it was, anyway."

"Did you ever see a wolf?" I ask him. He shakes his head no: the government killed all the wolves on the creek eighty years ago, before he even knew what to look for.

"I think I'd like to hear that old wolf again," he says. "Before I die, I'd really like to see one. I've been running cattle on this river since God made it, and I think that old lobo belongs here."

He's been looking for them for years, scanning this boulder-strewn canyon for their sign, not far downstream from the higher country where Aldo Leopold took the green fire out of a she-wolf's eyes a century ago, not so far downstream from the places where government biologists first released eleven gray wolves—three adult males, three adult females, three female pups and yearlings, and two male pups—from three acclimation pens within the seven thousand-square-mile, federally designated Blue Range Wolf Recovery Area in the summer of 1998.

I have been looking here, too, for six years now, combing the Mogollon Rim country to see whether the wolves have wandered down from the highlands. I have been on their trail from the start. I had written a book about wolves and several pieces of journalism about their reintroduction, and therefore passed as something of an expert. When the wolves were first released, the Discovery Channel thus sent me to report on their where-abouts, with the hope, I imagine, that some thrilling on-the-hunt tale would ensue. The reality was much tamer: I hooked up for a week with a group of government biologists following the transmitter-equipped wolves with what appeared to be some pretty Rube Goldbergesque radio-teleme-try equipment, the most advanced piece of which looked like nothing so much as a dowser's divining rod. But even with science on our side, we turned up no wolves in the flesh; they were smart enough to keep out of the way of nosy humans, even if we could see them beeping on the mon-itor and found piles of their poop from time to time.

What I turned up instead was plenty of high hopes on the part of those biologists, who had been working on the reintroduction for a decade and were visibly excited by the fact that wolves were now on the ground and keeping their distance—for these wolves were used to humans and needed to learn the wild art of running away from Homo sapiens. I turned up plenty of resistance on the part of local people, too. Some feared an assault on their livelihoods, based on the ever more marginal enterprise of cattle raising in land too poor to sustain those always hungry critters. More, it seemed, believed that the wolves were agents of the black helicopter/ United Nations/Trilateral Commission crowd, nefarious characters who had selected the people of the Mogollon Rim as the subjects of some espe-cially torturous experiment in one-worldism.

In that scenario, the capital of that conquered territory is the little town of Alpine, Arizona, the settlement closest to the Blue Range Recovery Area. Such habitations are scarce here, the chief reason that the wolves were released here in the first place, precisely in order "to minimize wolf-human interaction," as the biologists put it; Apache and Greenlee counties, the Arizona districts into which the area falls, are together larger than the state of Massachusetts, but their aggregate population is fewer than twenty thou-sand.

Alpine may be small, a blip on the road from nowhere to nowhere, but its residents were very much aware of the larger world. As I sat in the Bear Wallow Café over coffee, indulging in the fine and not especially taxing art of "enterprise journalism"—that is, go and sit somewhere and drink cof-fee or beer and listen for the Big Story—they talked about trading horses and repairing battered pickups and tolerating tourists from the city who pulled in to ask about property values and vacation-home amenities, but they also talked knowingly of the latest scandals embroiling then-President

Bill Clinton and debated the merits of various internet service providers: "Juno gives you free email, don't they?" a no-nonsense waitress asked one of them, who nodded in the affirmative.

That larger world, several residents of Alpine told me, was bringing them nothing but trouble. The Mexican gray wolves and their attendant government biologists were one thing; hot on their heels had come another source of grief, advance scouts for the Rainbow Family, a loose-knit, multi-generational clan of hippies whose annual gatherings in national forests across the West typically draw 30,000 attendants, there for dope, music, and cosmic brotherhood. The Rainbow people had heard about the wolves, it seems, and they thought it a pretty groovy thing to commune with them in the nearby national forest: wild people mounting a canid-friendly Wood-stock out in the boonies.

One afternoon I went to visit with a blacksmith and fix-it man who had been holding cracker-barrel seminars in constitutional law at the general store, preparing the people of Alpine for the revolution. He stared at a ragtag trio of Rainbow Family types, all tattered jeans and halter tops, with a mixture of disgust and curiosity, then sent a stream of tobacco juice onto the highway and smiled at me with genuine friendliness. "Well, they seem all right to me," he said. "A little dirty, maybe, but pretty well-mannered."

Known locally as "the mayor of the rednecks," the blacksmith was slight and rail-thin but looked as if he could wrestle any three humans—or wolves—single-handed. But, for all the violent rhetoric that sometimes swirls around the anti-environmentalist crowd in the West, he wasn't fixing to fight; a well-read, lively man who seemed to thrive on reasoned debate, he was just as happy to bat around words in the manner of his favorite writer, Winston Churchill. (Urbanites take note: country folks can be plenty sophisticated.) On the matter of wolf reintroduction, he had much to say; it was he who had organized local opposition to the reintroduction effort, he who had organized a rally that made national news on the day then-Interior Secretary Bruce Babbitt passed through Alpine to release the wolves from their pens. "We had our signs out," he said, "but the secretary went through here with a police escort at about seventy miles an hour. He ducked when he passed by, so I don't think he saw us. Probably a good thing, too."

"My bitterness about the wolf reintroduction program isn't so much with the wolves themselves," he continued. "Hell, I like wolves, what I know of them. It's with how the government brought them to us. The people around here were willing to give the wolf a try. We just didn't like the way the government brought it down on us. And we didn't think much of the government people to begin with. They don't know the country; if it had been up to me, I would have made them ride the range on horseback for a couple of weeks so they could see what this place is all about."

And then he came to the pay-dirt, smoking-gun heart of the matter.

"They should have had more local involvement from the beginning, maybe given some of the local people jobs surveying the wolves, building the pens, and so on," he said. "If they had, things would have been a lot smoother. But instead, they released the wolves too close to civilization, so now we get wolves in our yards, chasing our cows and attacking our dogs. It wasn't fair to the wolves, and it wasn't fair to us."

I hadn't heard anything about cow-chasing or dog-baiting from anyone else in Alpine, but there it was. Local sentiment may have been overwhelmingly antiwolf in a generalized kind of way, but the real problem was that the wolves worked for the government. Not so long ago, that very government had busily been exterminating them, but now they had been pressed into service in a war that has been raging for a long time, one in which the wolves were only an afterthought: the ancient conflict between yeomen and nobles. For its part, the nobility called the government—that great abstraction, filled with abstract thinkers—hadn't bothered to ask local people, the yeomen, how they felt, and worse, had made no effort to make local people a part of the process. (Please take note, planners of the future.) Well, it wasn't the first time the government behaved stupidly. And, as in the countryside just about everywhere, out in the outback of Arizona, never mind homage to the flag and yellow ribbons for the troops, the government was perceived as the enemy, and an unthinking enemy at that.

Not involving the people of Alpine amounted to a king-sized missed opportunity, for besides the mayor-at-large, many of the people of Alpine allowed that they had no trouble with the wolves themselves. Over at the Bear Wallow, I asked a middle-aged woman what she thought of the whole business, and she said, "I make the drive down the mountain every day. I see lots of animals—deer and elk, mostly, and sometimes bears and mountain lions. I don't mind seeing the wolves here, too." A couple of tables away, another woman, a native of "the mountain," as its residents call the area, called for another cup of coffee, turned to me, and whispered, "I'm one of the few locals who wants the wolves here. But don't tell anyone, all right?" And a man born and raised on the mountain said, "I think those of us who live here ought to all become greennecks, and I bet 30 percent of the people here would say they're in favor of reintroducing the wolf. But you can get your house burned down for saying so, and so people don't." He preferred to remain anonymous.

So do the wolves. Inconvenient children in an ugly divorce, victims of political abstractions, us-against-them sloganeering, and absolutely real bullets, many have died at human hands since 1998, hunted down by shooters without the advantage of radio-telemetry equipment but with a deep-seated interest in thwarting the designs of the federal government. But other wolves have been born, and the slowly increasing Blue Range clan has fanned out into country that nineteenth-century explorers reckoned to be among the roughest and wildest on earth, making the deep forests the center of their partisan activities.

They are out there, to be sure, out in the land of Cochise and Geronimo. They are out there, and whenever I venture into the ponderosa forest, just a little distance away from the highway that switchbacks down to the desert far below, I like to think that I can feel their eyes on me, like to think that they see me as a friend, or at least not an enemy. I'm not sure that they would trust the distinction, given their experience, but I have reason to be sure of their presence: once, across a clearing below 9,300-foot Blue Peak, I saw a shape—merely the suggestion of a shape, really—that could have been nothing other than a wolf, studying me as I picked my way over the broken boulders to get a closer look, then turning and melting—poof! just like that—into the dark woods, as if to say, maybe next time, maybe some day.

And so I have been looking for *Canis lupus,* working the canyons and mountains, contenting myself with the occasional clump of scat, with the occasional scattering of rabbit bones and fur, with negative evidence and arguments from silence.

No, not contenting myself. It is not enough for me to think that maybe, just maybe, some wolf somewhere has been fortunate enough to escape a bullet that is still relentlessly on the hunt for it, has merely lived another day.

I will be an old man soon enough, wiping my brow in the desert light, teary-eyed, searching out ghosts and memories of my own. I am weary of abstractions, of rants against Washington and Washington reports alike. Before I leave this place, I would like to see something more than a single distant gray shape in the forest, would like to hear that medulla-quickening howl in country whose music has been the poorer for lack of it. I want to witness a genuine resurrection. I want the wolves to come home. We have just that possibility: in Arizona, in Colorado, in the mountain corridors of the West and across the continent, it is within our means to undo at least some of the untold damage we have done to this generous land. The Blue Range is only a start. We have a world to win.

Rick Bass

Rick Bass, a widely published novelist and essayist, has been on the trail of wolves, bears, and other denizens of the Rocky Mountains for many years. His book The Ninemile Wolves *traces the fortunes of one reintroduced pack in Montana, where Bass lives. In this essay, Bass considers the fortunes of another group preparing for reintroduction in the southern portion of the range.*

Anything for Hope

Six years ago, in 1998, we camped—wolf watchers, students, and volunteers—on one of Ted Turner's big New Mexico ranches. It's a dry landscape, sere, with most of its color locked in the frozen embrace of the rocks. Grama grass waves in the wind, and the granitic hills are dotted sparsely with yucca, sotol, mesquite, and juniper. Oaks, cottonwoods, and sycamores grow giant and shady along the creeks. Visible to the west lie New Mexico's Gila National Forest and Arizona's Blue River range, where Mexican wolves were soon to be released. How did the creature that was once the most widely distributed mammal in the world become the rarest? The old-fashioned way: guns and poison.

Cattle flooded the Southwest in the late 1800s and early 1900s. Coyotes had occupied the grasslands and valley bottoms, while the wolves had preferred the cooler, higher country of forests and mountains. But then wolves came down to avail themselves to those huge cattle herds—herds trampling the land, herds rerouting and devastating the rivers, until the rivers ran dry. Wolves came down out of the mountains like some hand or finger of God trying to counter the shock of what was being done to the land by the Eastern bankers who just kept dumping the cattle on, not understanding or caring. And that is the story of the American West since whites hit it: liquidation of public resources by venture capitalists; ecological theft, generation after generation; and once the wolves became hooked on beef, they were easy to target. The wolves used familiar, traditional runways, making trapping easy, and so used had they become to eating dead cattle and other livestock that ranchers had only to sprinkle poison into a carcass and then come back the next day, or the next, to find a ring of dead and dying wolves radiating outward from that source of poison. As has been well documented, the government got in on the act and subsidized the eradication of every last wolf in the Southwest, spreading across generations, across cultures, the idea that wolves were vermin.

By 1905, wolves were scarce in the Southwest. By 1960, there were only the rarest observations. Each wolf found trapped or poisoned was thought surely to be "the last wolf." But in 1976, the government had finally changed its mind. It listed the subspecies as endangered and hired trapper Roy McBride to go catch all he could for a captive breeding program. He found eight. In 1998, there were about 175 wolves in the program—all behind bars, but not for long.

On those original eight, plus a few more individuals from down in Mexico, an entire subspecies banked its fate, and then in one of history's typical pendulum swings, money was being spent trying to recover the wolves.

∼

The recovery plan called for the wolves to be kept in a kind of halfway house during the acclimatization process. At first the plan was for pens to be constructed on the Apache-Sitgreaves National Forest, but the security concerns would have been a nightmare, as would have been the political fallout of "locking up" public lands.

So Ted Turner stepped in. His ranch is not too far from the Blues—similar country, with similar elevations—and he offered to house the wolves. The Turner Endangered Species Fund, supported on this particular project by the Turner Foundation, footed the bill. A cynic might say they did it for the public relations value, an optimist might say they did it for reasons of democracy or even spirit, and a pragmatist might say they did it for all of the above, or somewhere in between. Personally, I just wanted the wolves to get out of captivity and to have their best shot. I don't think any of us is any purer than anyone else. The capitalist savagery of Pegasus Gold and Anaconda Copper, the bone-crushing indifference and the mindless insatiability of the timber companies, and the spinelessness of government—these things make me rail—but I've eaten a French fry or two at McDonald's, I've flown on a jet, ridden in a car, and traded and bartered with the currency of the land. I need wilderness, big wilderness, as an antidote to my sins, a place to say, *Here I will finally devour nothing,* and I really need those wolves to make it, despite the longest of odds. All that stuff is behind the wave, anyway, and already has fallen into dim history and dust. The forward momentum of the wolves, and the space they have occupied, is what we are looking at, out in front of us, out in the near future. So we camped by a creek beneath giant cottonwoods and listened to their leaf-rattle all night, and to the slow trillings of crickets, the yappings of coyotes, and the gruntings of javelinas. The ranch set up crisp big tents for the volunteers, so that it looked, I suppose, like some African safari. The volunteers were fed, and for that they had to work, preparing a place and a way for the coming of the wolves.

Our project director, Tom Savage, wanted to do everything by hand. No cement mixers, no bulldozers: just human beings. The five holding pens were constructed on steep south-facing slopes to help the wolves get used to the warmth and to encourage them to dig dens. At the tops of the steep pens—each about a third of an acre in size—was a level area where the wolves were to be fed and, when necessary, tended to by a vet. Entire freezers of gutted, roadkilled deer and elk awaited the wolves' dining experience; for two years prior to that day, an AmeriCorps volunteer prowled the American Southwest, gathering wild game from the roadside ditches, in anticipation. The thawing began soon thereafter. Frozen elk melted back into meat for the wolves: motionless meat, no meat on the hoof, but a start nonetheless. Blocks of frozen deer melted, and the fenced-in wolves, frozen in captivity for seven generations, finally melted back out onto the landscape.

I knew the odds were long. Extraordinarily long, it seemed to me, some days. But being around the young students and volunteers and seeing their work on the physical actualities of the release—seeing something you could touch with your hand, a thing of heft, of specific density, namely, the release pens—did wonders for my hope. The project was going forward. The time for too much worry was all in the past, and energy poorly spent, at that. As we camped, the wolves were coming, and being around these young people, I got the feeling that they couldn't be stopped.

∾

A brilliant sunrise, the world sheeted in frost. I was hard-pressed to pin down exactly what we felt, but it was good. We stood around the nearly eternal campfire, warming our feet, waiting. There was a sense of relaxed eagerness, so to speak—pleasure and pride, among the students, at having done a job well, and the pleasure and pride of having completed something; and this in turn was tempered, bounced, by the knowledge that their completion was another thing's beginning.

What is the heft, the density, of correctness—of authenticity? It's satisfying that we can still recognize it when we encounter it, even if a finite definition eludes us.

We finished our tea and oatmeal, and started up the dry canyon in single file. A canyon wren sang to us as we traveled up the cobbled canyon, passing between the hulks of leafless cottonwoods—the dried brown and yellow leaves rustling against our boots. At one point we leaped across a wide stretch of stream, and we stumbled with early-morning awkwardness and stiff cold feet across that mossy, loose-rock crossing, splashing and clattering like cattle. We bushwhacked through a copse of drying cattails, and plumes of cattails exploded in puffs skyward, floating seeds spiraling upward around us, illuminating all around us in the winter sun like candle tapers. We were all coated instantly with seed-wrack, and cloaked in gold light, as the fine drift of cattail puff glowed incandescent. Seeds in our hair, on our arms and coats, clinging to our boots: the dispersers. Agents of dispersal.

We pushed on up the canyon, a part of the landscape, carrying those seeds to new crevices, new veins of soil, where they might or might not find purchase.

As we peered down behind us, the pens looked as if they had been there forever. The rusting fences were nearly invisible, as Tom had planned and hoped. The neat stone walls were pleasing: they did not disrupt the view, did not disrupt anything.

We eased up over the stony bluff, gathered around the observation booth up on the ridge a few hundred yards away, and watched Tom and his associate release the four new wolves into the two new pens. These wolves were selected for genetic redundancy, so that if they vanished, they would not represent a loss to the genetic variability of the world's tiny population. Computer dating.

Anything for freedom. Anything for hope, for chance.

I'm not aware of worshipping individual animals, or species. My affinity, my allegiance, is with complete landscapes, and wild places. I'd rather try to protect an undesignated wilderness area—a landscape's wild qualities, which comprise ten billion variables—than spend energy on shopping or lobbying for the return of some single species—a grizzly, a wolf, a caribou. You can go out and buy a wolf and set it down in that lacking landscape, but the next morning, your problems—the landscape's problems—are still going to be the same. You can travel up to Canada or Alaska and capture one of the wild things in that country and bring it down to some other place, as if merely consuming, or shopping, to fill in the emotional blanks of a fractured landscape. In such instances, you have often changed nothing of substance but have merely gratified yourself. The wolves, or grizzlies, are like an echo of your need, while your real need, the land itself—the wild land—remains imperiled, vanishing.

That said, I was not prepared for what I felt when I saw the wolves enter, or reenter, their new world.

Tom swung open the gate to the portable kennel and the first wolf glided out like smoke, and yet as real, as vital, as any animal I had ever seen. This animal was not yet smoke, memory, anecdote, I thought, and then I wondered, was it my imagination, or had the compression of a race, a subspecies, down to these last hundred-plus individuals, imbued each individual somehow with an increased density of spirit, increased responsibility? Nothing less than two million years of carving rested on this one wolf, and a few others, that bright winter day.

The yellow-green eyes of fire caught the sunlight and glowed. It was the larger wolf, the male, who was out first. Even though he was a bit soft-looking, not yet possessing the electric muscle tone of a creature living in the wild, he was one of the most beautiful animals I'd ever seen. We stared at him with nothing less than hunger, watching every move: the confidence of each joint's articulation, the confidence of muzzle taking in new scent, the confidence of being alive in the world.

Those yellow-green eyes: everything they have is in those eyes, as you or I might pack everything we have into a storage shed, or the back of a truck. Their eyes carry more than ours do. We are children, looking into those eyes—we have been here such a short time, while they have been here so long. Who are we to consider saving *them?*

The male trotted immediately toward the fence, made a couple of passes up and down it, then crouched and relieved himself.

The female came out. She was spryer, wilder—she flared from the handlers, skittered away as if windblown.

She made straight for where the male scent-marked, paused, then began digging at that spot and sniffing at it. Later, she rubbed her back against that place, as if she couldn't get enough of that soil.

The other two were released into a second pen. The male came right on out, but the female wouldn't exit; and even when her cage, her kennel, was picked up and held open over the ground—like trying to shake out the last kernels of popcorn from a paper bag—she would not come out. Inside, she must've had all four legs braced against the inside of the kennel's walls. Again, the kennel was shaken, held upside down, and finally she skirted out and ran promptly for the pen's boundaries.

Such avoidance behavior—coming especially from the females—was pleasing to all.

For the next hour and a half, we watched the wolves explore their new homes. The first couple—downward from the other wolves—seemed more comfortable with their enclosure and their fellow wolves. Soon they played with each other: crouched, pounced, teased.

The second couple, however, appeared more tense. All the wolves were the same age—one year, eight months. It was so strange to see smack in front of us the physical evidence of recombination—both males from one captive breeding site, both females from another—with such varying, seemingly random responses. One pen, frisky; another pen, tense.

As we watched, the weight of responsibility began to settle with something closer to its full weight. Humans would be doing the weaving, and reweaving, for a little while—helping to set back in motion that which we nearly extinguished.

It seemed so important that we succeed.

Jerry, a volunteer standing next to me, was transfixed with his binoculars, as were all the students.

"Just think," he said quietly. "Every dog in the world—all the different breeds—comes from that one creature." He nodded down at the wolves, who were still examining their new quarters with ceaseless curiosity. This was the ultimate contract. We bedded down with them two million years ago. In one sense, we have sculpted them—dogs—from the rootstock of wolves: Jack Russell terriers, French poodles, black labs, all dogs—but on the larger, longer scale, they have been sculpting us, who we are, and who we will become, since even before we were here. Helping sculpt the *idea* of us, and the space for us, before we even arrived.

I was aware that humans were the ones doing the weaving—choosing which new wolf to recombine with which other one—but up there on the bluff, as their graceful movements held us spellbound, it seemed surely that the wolves were in charge. Wherever they went, whatever they did, we were going to watch them; we could not look away. Some fabric was being woven in the air between them and us—our sight, the thread, and their movements, the needles.

The male in the first pen squatted and urinated on another patch of open soil near the fence; the female soon wandered over to investigate that spot, dug there for a while, then writhed in the soil at that spot. That new spot.

Jets of cold morning frost-breath leaped from all four wolves' mouths as they paced. Small birds flocked toward the junipers as if to greet them—the next spring, perhaps, those birds' nests would be lined with tufts of wolf fur—and then swirled away.

Whenever the wolves stopped pacing for a moment—to follow with their eyes the nimbus of passing birds; to study the sky for the source of a lone raven's croak—they seemed to vanish. The color of the wheat-toned grama grass on the hillside was the exact hue of their coats, painted in that rich coppery light; in all their years of captivity, they had not lost that.

From behind the next ridge, over in another pen, one of the other wolves—knowing surely of their arrival, despite being upwind—began to howl. When he first cut loose it startled the little female in the first pen, made her flinch.

As we listened to that howl echo off the rock bluffs—the howler carried on for eight minutes, punctuating his howls with barks—there was no one among us who did not believe the wolves would make it.

Jack Collom

Jack Collom lives in Boulder, Colorado, and has for many years taught ecological creative writing at Naropa University. Among his books is Red Car Goes By: Selected Poems 1955–2000. With just two simple words, this poem offers a remarkably concise image of the wolf's legendary lope.

That Lobo Lope

```
W                       W                                       W
   O              O        O                          O
      L      L              L         L
         F                       F
W                       W                                       W
   O              O        O                          O
      L      L              L         L
         F                       F
W                       W                                       W
   O              O        O                          O
      L      L              L         L
         F                       F
```

Rob Edward

Rob Edward is the director of Sinapu's carnivore restoration program and one of the fourteen members of the Colorado Wolf Working Group. A native of Idaho who now lives in Boulder, Rob has dedicated his professional life to conservation and human rights issues. In this essay, he describes his own life as an activist and tells part of the story of the return of wolves to Colorado and the southern Rockies.

Howling Back

The television image brightens from black to a shadowy, old-growth forest. As glimpses of a wolf moving through the undergrowth flash nervously through the scene—giving a sense of impending doom—a female's voice drones darkly: "In an increasingly dangerous world, even after the first terrorist attack on America, John Kerry and the liberals in Congress voted to slash America's intelligence budget by $6 billion, cuts so deep they would have weakened America's defenses." The scene switches to several wolves resting on a hillside, until the observer apparently catches their attention and they rise to give chase. The female announcer continues, "And weakness attracts those who are waiting to do America harm." As the ad fades to black, the voice of President George W. Bush announces his approval of the piece.

Turning off the television, I stood staring blankly at the darkening screen. The ad's not-so-subtle use of wolves as a metaphor for terrorists left me dumbfounded. Yet the Bush Administration had never proven to be a friend to wolves. In fact, Secretary of the Interior Gail Norton—a Bush appointee—approached her stewardship of the nation's wolves much like a princess would approach a stinky shirt. This ad, however, was a cheap shot. After nearly a decade of struggling to build the scientific case and a constituency for wolves in the southern Rockies, I felt my blood boil at this ad. The political hacks who created it were so proud of themselves they granted interviews to the major media outlets just to discuss their handiwork. They argued that the ad's imagery "tested as very compelling with focus groups."

I knew that my righteous indignation wouldn't stop the ad from airing, however. This felt like familiar territory.

~

In early 1995, just a few months after I had arrived in Boulder, Colorado, the Republican-controlled House of Representatives took up the mantle of the logging and livestock industries, crafting a bill to suspend environmental laws that govern these industries on public lands. Facing this unprecedented opportunity, industry lobbyists twisted many important arms in the Capitol. Despite their efforts, however, as the bill came to a vote it appeared as if the Senate would rebuke the House version by a one-vote margin. Regrettably, Colorado's Senator Ben Nighthorse Campbell switched his vote, giving a green light to the "lawless logging bill"; within weeks, the U.S. Forest Service had several massive tracts of pristine western forest up for sale.

Incensed by this betrayal of the last fragments of America's wild forests, thousands of citizens in the western United States took to the streets in protest. Although similar provisions to suspend environmental review of livestock grazing were equally pernicious, images of chainsaws raging in America's wilderness sparked the most outrage.

By the summer of 1995, that outrage drove me—once a Republican—to chain myself to four of my friends atop the roof of the Colorado Republican Party headquarters in Denver. Hundreds of people milled around in the streets below, chanting songs for the forests, waving signs and banners and doing their best to ensure that the people of Colorado knew there was trouble in paradise.

For several hours, we remained atop the building, giving the local papers enough time to take a few good pictures—and allowing the police time to figure out how to cut the bike locks binding us together. Even before the police and fire department had removed us from the roof, the crowd below had successfully raised our bail by simply passing the hat. Nonetheless, the police held us for eleven hours and subjected us to an unrelenting barrage of sarcasm.

None of us believed that we'd single-handedly move our government to restore law to our public lands. Like the millions of citizens of this country who'd risked their freedom in decades past to protest injustices, we still felt obliged to bear witness to this latest insult. Bearing witness comes at a price, however, and this particularly nasty battle had left me running on fumes.

∼

A few months after our brief stay on top of the Republican headquarters, I fled from Boulder to the Little Piedra River in the San Juan Mountains of southwestern Colorado, hoping to reinvigorate myself. I knew that the sound of the river sliding over timeworn rocks, the wind hissing through the ancient ponderosas, and the warm smell of the forest floor would cleanse my political wounds. Basking in the hospitality of this natural spa, I hoped to regain the clarity I'd come to Colorado with only two years before.

Plodding in a daze along the narrowing bank, I let my sadness for nature flow out of my soul in pace with the river. I moved a few steps farther and the cold slate walls of the canyon pressed into the water. Just beyond, the river turned sharply left, diverted by a monolithic slab of rock. I paused a moment in reverence of this stunning cathedral, and then wandered back toward my camp guided by shards of tree-broken light.

For hours, I remained rapt in the chorus of wind and water. Finally, a primal urge to make my presence known gripped me. As the sun dipped behind the canyon walls, I cocked my head back and howled. A long, throaty bawl shot up from my toes and burst into the canyon. I waited. Again, I reached back into the primitive recesses of my brain and cast forth a mournful cry. Clarity. That's what I'd come here for. With my third raspy yowl, I felt my body shake. I dropped to the forest floor on my hands and knees, duff and dirt grinding into my skin.

Clarity. I bawled again. Not all that far from here Colorado's last wolf had perished in 1945, killed by a government trapper. Beckoning the ghosts of those last wolves, I yearned to hear their refrain, their answer to my summons. Silence was the only reply.

∼

Some of my friends and family might call me a chronic activist. It started in my late twenties with a stint advocating for whales off the coast of Boston. Then I moved on to Arizona to herd sheep for Navaho elders resisting relocation from the reservation. Finally, in late 1994, I settled down to join the staff of a grassroots group called Sinapu, named after the Ute word for wolves. As its name hints, the group aims to repatriate wolves to the hunting grounds of their ancestors in the Colorado high country. The starting pay was only slightly better than the sheepherding gig (free), but the public's intense interest in the organization's goals made it feel like a good fit.

Unfortunately, shortly after I arrived in Boulder, Congress's lawless logging shenanigans created a political and legal quagmire that sapped the energy, money, and enthusiasm of the nation's conservation groups and their millions of supporters; for the time being, wolves had to take a back seat to forest defense. Staring into the abyss of that political reality made clear the long road ahead. Sinapu needed to forge a compelling argument for wolf restoration in the southern Rocky Mountains to reinvigorate the interest of the big groups like Defenders of Wildlife and the Sierra Club. Thus, I dedicated the next several years to meticulously laying a credible scientific and political underpinning for that argument.

Though perhaps it is simplistic to think of wolves as victims of a social phenomenon, indeed they were. The phenomenon, which the influential American editor John O'Sullivan called "Manifest Destiny" in 1845, rolled over wolves, bison, bears, and native peoples like a hurricane. Pushed by a swelling immigrant population and the promise of "free" land, Manifest Destiny thundered across the American landscape, transforming once wild lands into pastoral countryside.

Bounties, poison, traps, and restless young men with guns and horses—these were the cruel winds of Manifest Destiny. They howled through wild America until she lay bare. Gone were the animals with sharp teeth and claws—and with them the cornerstones of the land's well-being. Though it would take the nation nearly a century to realize the implications of this radical transformation of the continent, visionaries like Aldo Leopold and John Muir presaged the outcome. Ultimately, Leopold's words would serve as a clarion call to the great-grandchildren of those who cleansed the continent of wolves, motivating them to stitch wolves back into the fabric of the American West.

I wonder what Leopold might think of this contemporary effort to give wolves a foothold in the West. Would he argue that it is too late? Would he bemoan the fact that wolves must now make a living among herds of cattle and sheep? Or, conversely, would he celebrate? Would he urge us on, pointing to all that we now know about the role that wolves play?

Just a few months before Congress freed the Forest Service of the burdens of environmental law, another branch of government had freed several packs of wolves in Wyoming and Idaho. Against the din of shrill criticism from western elected officials and a few vocal ranchers and hunters, the West's repatriated wolves were busy changing the landscape.

Like a potter at the wheel turning a block of clay into beauty, wolves were reshaping the territories of resident coyote clans, remolding the behavior of elk and deer, and in turn sculpting the countryside. Aspen and willows—withering under decades of grazing by sedentary elk, deer, and moose—rebounded as elk and deer moved more frequently under the pressure of resident wolves. With more young trees cropping up, beaver began to reclaim stretches of local streams. Their dams quickly gave rise to new wetlands—and thus habitat for songbirds, insects, and fish. A few years into this momentous experiment, scientific journals and the popular media would begin marveling at the big ripples wolves were sending through their homeland.

Undaunted by the magic that wolves were working, the livestock industry and a few angry hunting associations continued to trot out time-worn myths. Wolves will decimate livestock herds. All of the elk and deer will be gone in a decade. Local economies will collapse. Children will disappear from bus stops.

Held up to the mirror of fact, these myths crumble. Where wolves and livestock share the land, wolves kill less than one in ten thousand cows and sheep each year. Weather kills scores more livestock in those same areas each year. Canada never eliminated wolves, yet the nation's hunting and ranching industries continue to thrive. Wolves (and many other carnivores) existed in significant numbers throughout North America before European conquest. How is it that these flesh-eating machines managed not to decimate their food supply before we came along to "manage" them?

Yet, in the face of the unrelenting cries of anti-wolf factions that "the sky is falling," we had our work cut out for us. We'd have to assemble a solid base of facts to counter the antiwolf rhetoric—and so, in the waning years of the 1990s, we did.

∿

As the 1990s ended, we had gathered enough preliminary evidence to suggest that Colorado would be a great place for wolves. As hoped, these findings sparked the interest of several scientists and national conservation groups and ultimately led to the formation of the Southern Rockies Wolf Restoration Project, a coalition of groups led by Sinapu and the Sierra Club.

By the spring of 2003, years of painstaking work to assemble the scientific case for wolves in Colorado paid off. Building upon the work of Sinapu and others, a team of world-renowned scientists published the results of an exhaustive study noting that Colorado's Rocky Mountains could support nearly a thousand wolves. This great news followed on the heels of a public opinion study that showed overwhelming support for restoring wolves to Colorado.

As the stars began to align for wolves in the Southern Rockies, the Bush administration attempted to put legal protections for wolves on a fast track to oblivion late in 2003. In response, Sinapu and many of our national partners joined forces to sue the government over their premature efforts to declare wolves as "recovered." Given our direct attack against the Bush administration's wolf policy, I suppose I shouldn't have been surprised when the reelection campaign for George W. Bush rolled out an ad on terrorism featuring wolves as the visual centerpiece.

Fortunately, despite its Orwellian overtones, the Bush campaign's wolf ad can't erase the tremendous progress that conservationists have made on behalf of wolves during the past decade. We've got the science and the good will of the public on our side. No longer can the government ignore the importance of the Southern Rocky Mountains for wolves. No longer can the livestock industry insist that there's no room for wolves in Colorado. No longer will the public accept the impoverished landscape as a given.

Recalling the sounds of the Little Piedra River, where I once howled my hopes to the wind, I wonder how near the day might be when I might finally hear an answer to that howl. The pulse of the land seems feeble in the silence. Still, the wild heart beats steadily, anticipating the refrain.

Stephen Trimble

Freelance writer and photographer Stephen Trimble grew up in Denver, attended Colorado College, and worked as a park ranger at Great Sand Dunes. His many books focus on homeland, wildland, and Indian land, including The Geography of Childhood: Why Children Need Wild Places *(with Gary Nabhan) and the forthcoming* Bargaining for Eden. *He speaks eloquently in this essay of the hope that wolves can bring with them as they return home.*

Wolfsong of Hope

Thirty-five years ago, I slept on a lumpy terrace of tundra above a glacial valley in the Snowmass Wilderness. Or tried to sleep. Even though my climbing buddies and I had seen just one black bear here in Colorado, even though we were hundreds of miles from grizzly country, the three of us managed to keep ourselves awake all night, an irrational fear of bears fueling our insomnia.

Colorado was a nearly toothless wilderness in those last decades of the twentieth century. The big predators weren't here. Grizzlies were reduced to tantalizing rumors of sightings drifting from deep within the San Juan Mountains. Colorado's wolves had all been killed before I was born. Cougars were here, but elusive.

Still, my friends and I cranked up the sense of danger by magnifying the threat posed by black bears who spent their summers grazing on berries. We knew wildness was incomplete without big predators, and we wanted the Southern Rockies to be truly wild—to echo with howling wolves, to smell like grizzlies fresh from their rank dens. We were thrilled and eager, for even in their expurgated state, these Southern Rockies were our first wilderness, our ceremonial space for coming of age.

Wilderness, for us, was an iconic place where animals kill one another, and, potentially, could kill us—a Rocky Mountain version of the Forests of the Night, where William Blake's "tygers" burned bright. We expected the compressed drama narrated by PBS, with its tightly edited Serengeti, but what we found was more like reels of raw footage, with fleeting glimpses and long waits and protagonists who had left the set. We had yet to grow comfortable with the intoxicating and provocative emotion bestowed by intimate encounters with wild creatures. The transparency, the humility, the vulnerability of looking into the eyes of our equals from other animal tribes—all required a maturity we did not have.

Years have passed. I've approached bull bison, judging their moods and preparing to bolt. I've camped in East African savanna where lions and elephants moved past our tent. I've been in a small boat in the open ocean, surrounded by a pod of blue whales misting the tropical sunset with their blows. I've surprised bobcats at sunrise and watched coyotes stalk ground squirrels. I know that in intact western wilderness, grizzlies pose a small, though real, threat and that mountain lions want deer, not mountain bikers.

With these experiences I understand a little more about why we need wild places with their full complement of species.

Aldo Leopold, our guide to living ethically with the land, learned to "think like a mountain" after he watched the "fierce green fire" die in the eyes of a wolf he had shot in the days when range biologists always shot wolves. He watched what happened to the mountain afterward, as unchecked deer herds reduced brush to bare ground, and then starved. The mountain suffered—and so the imagined safety that deer, elk, moose, and cattle might enjoy free from wolves proved illusory.

Nearly sixty years ago, Leopold taught us in *A Sand County Almanac* that our mountains are incomplete when they have lost their wolves. Modern conservation biologists reinforce his argument for maintaining populations of keystone species that interact with whole ecosystems—restoring the links in food chains, mending holes in the fabric of biodiversity. If we can't learn to think like our home mountains, we are doomed to destroy them.

And so when wolves came home to Yellowstone, I rejoiced. And I dreamed.

In my dream, I was picnicking with my family on the banks of a Yellowstone river. We sat on sun-warmed cobbles under a small cutbank, reveling in the clarity of the light, the cold strength of the current, and the love in our family. These phrases sound corny, but a sense of well-being suffused my dream.

Suddenly a body full of grace and strength leapt from the bank and arched slowly over us—a wolf bounding across the sky. The animal hovered longer than it would in life, taking its time, a canopy of fur ruffling and muscle rippling, finally landing—close—at water's edge. The big predator felt completely benevolent—but Other, Wild. I awoke, astonished and exultant.

The dream is now reality in Yellowstone, in the Northern Rockies. As we introduce our children to wild places—even as the wild places disappear—wolves accompany us. Seen or unseen, wolves have returned, to call in a chorus of wildness that still raises the hackles on our necks. We no longer have to pass on myths that twist the wolf—a smart predator with a rich social life and fierce loyalty—into Evil, into the Devil, into the rapacious Big Bad Wolf. We know the truth: wolf packs don't attack people. We can replace the imaginary animal with a real one.

Greater Yellowstone is a superlative, a refuge, a place for pilgrimage. If we restore wolves to our backyard mountains here in the Colorado Rockies, we rebuild our connections to wildness even more profoundly than if we harbor packs only within the sanctuaries of national parks.

I can already hear the howl, the chorus, the wolfsong of hope, when we bring the wild wolves home.

Pattiann Rogers

Recipient of many awards and fellowships, Pattiann Rogers, who lives in Castle Rock, Colorado, is the author of eleven books, including Generations *and* Song of the World Becoming: New and Collected Poems, 1981-2001. *In this poem from the second volume, she speaks for the many of us who have never seen a wild wolf and so must imagine them instead: like this coyote in the city, our wolves are often present in the sheer power of their absence.*

Creation by the Presence of Absence: City Coyote in Rain

She's sleek blue neon through
the blue of the evening. She's black
sheen off the blue of wet streets,
blue daunt of suspension in each
pendant of rain filling the poplars
on the esplanade.

Her blue flank flashes once in the panes
of empty windows as she passes.
She's faster than lighthouse blue
sweeping the seas in circles.

Like the leaping blue of flames
burning in an alley barrel, her presence
isn't perceived until she's gone.

She cries with fat blue yelps, calls
with the scaling calls of the ragmen,
screeches a siren of howls along the docks
below the bridges, wails with the punctuated
griefs of drunks and orphans.

She scuttles under gates, through doors
hanging by broken hinges, behind ash
bins, into a culvert, shakes off the storm
in an explosion of radiance, licks
the cold muzzles and genitals of her frenzied
pups, gives them her blue teats, closes
her yellow eyes.

No one ever sees her face to face,
or those who do never know they do,
denying her first, preempting her lest
the place of pattern and time she creates,
like the blue of a star long since
disintegrated, enter their hearts
with all of its implications.

Gary Wockner

Gary Wockner is an environmental writer and ecologist living in Fort Collins, Colorado. Author of the novel Bicycle Cowboy.com, *he did his PhD research on wolf management at Isle Royale National Park and serves as a wildlife advocate on the Colorado Wolf Working Group. Here he writes as a parent who discovers the wild wolf—and the hope it represents—in unexpected places.*

Soccer Dads for Gray Wolves

We are driving through the south side of Denver on I–25 on the way to our oldest daughter's soccer game. We left Fort Collins about two hours ago, and right now we are bunched up in a traffic jam here on Saturday morning amidst a horde of idling, belching beasts—bumper-to-bumper cars and trucks as far as I can see in front and in the opposing northbound lane. This year our family graduated from the "Intermediate" soccer league to the "Arsenal" league, and thus the minivan gets fueled up and the soc-cer-road-warrior-mom-and-dad step into high parental-travel mode.

We are surrounded by cement—the road below, the overpasses above, and on both sides of the interstate. To our left and right are twelve-foot-high cement sound barriers and cement walls separating the highway from nearby neighborhoods. It's got a *Blade Runner* feel, a postmodern industrial craziness, a soupy amalgam of automobile-Americana that uniquely dis-plays the paradox between our always moving minds and down-to-earth geography.

As we inch along near mile marker 205, the scenery suddenly changes. The strip of sky above our cement tunnel is that brilliant Colorado blue and the sun is plastering the cement with a healthy golden-gray reflection, and in that reflection rises an apparition. This urban canyon is covered with pictures and shapes of nature. The folks who built this slipstream thorough-fare molded and etched the cement walls into tree leaves, vines, huge fly-ing swallows, and mountain pictographs. The swallows, in particular, are car-sized and intricately etched into the cement. These images are gray and motionless, to be sure, but beautiful in their own cement way, a kind of twenty-first-century cave art. I am bedazzled.

In an earlier stage of life, I would have interpreted these images differently, as a kind of simulation, an ironic and distasteful facsimile of the wild. We are inundated with such ironies, the most obvious of which is that the land below this interstate was likely once home to the wildness—the trees, vines, and swallows—pictured on these walls. In a sour mood, I might have envisioned a Blade Runner future where these wall etchings were in full color, or maybe contained the video projections of a forest (with appropriate corporate endorsement every other block) to give us the feel of traveling elsewhere instead of this urban tunnel. Surely these cement etchings are the first step in that direction, the wool that we are ever more interested in pulling over our eyes as we smother the landscape below.

As if on cue to nudge me into a more hopeful future as we putter along the interstate, a car pulls in front of ours with a Wisconsin license plate. I ease up to its bumper as we stop-and-go through this sculpted trench. The license plate catches my eye, an image I am familiar with, showing the picture of a wolf and these words below the image, "Endangered Resources." And with this image, my optimism rises to the surface.

Several years back, Wisconsin gave its residents the option to pay an extra twenty-five dollars per year for a special license plate to help pay for and save endangered resources, the wolf in particular. The program has been a huge success. It has raised millions of dollars and the wolf is proliferating across Wisconsin's north woods. When I lived in Wisconsin, the "wolf license plate" was everywhere, at bumper level, cruising around the state's highways and backroads. Drivers defined themselves through this image, and by this image were able to take a material stance, to make an actual payment for the very thing, not the image, they hoped to perpetuate—wolves and other endangered species.

I remember seeing similarly used images everywhere in my daily life as a wildlife advocate—wildlife books that donate to wildlife causes, photo-calendars that donate to open-lands movements, and the ubiquitous wildlife-cause T-shirt. And now I see a similar purpose in the cement etchings along the road. In a very bright mood, I can imagine a host of other images, an alternative future that is not a simulation but a wool sweater (predator friendly) that we pull over our eyes and down over our bodies to keep warm all winter.

Here along I-25, in the most unlikely of places, I am surrounded by images of nature. I believe I know why. As our family slowly drives through here, the conversation inside the van livens up. My two daughters, aged eight and ten, sit in the back and start meticulously viewing and analyzing the cave art.

"That one's got big wings," says my older daughter about a particularly huge etching of a swallow. "It's flying right into that mountain."

"Look at those vines," says my younger daughter. "They look like ivy."

"No," says the older girl, "they're more like pumpkin leaves."

"Too small," the younger girl responds, "and plus, look at the stem. It's more like ivy."

"Why do you always see swallows at road intersections?" asks the older daughter. And with that, the conversation complicates and veers into a nature lesson in which my wife takes an honest stab at answering that and other questions.

A few minutes later and the conversation turns to the wolf license plate in front of us. My younger daughter, who was born in Wisconsin, is particularly interested in why this animal is on that license plate, and as I answer her question, she becomes even more interested in what Wisconsin does with the money it collects. The questions and answers get a little more complicated, and then slowly, the conversation turns to Colorado's efforts to deal with wolf management and my role in that process. The girls know I'm on the Colorado Wolf Working Group, and so whenever the subject of wolves comes up, the topic turns to Colorado's efforts to support and reintroduce wolves. We spend a few minutes going over the story and I give them a distilled explanation that brushes on some abstractions like "endangered species" and "wildness." Fortunately, they've seen wild wolves in Yellowstone, and so they know real animals live behind the abstract words.

I certainly don't try to drum anything into these girls' heads, but they listen intently and overhear, and they know I'm a strong advocate for wolves. They also know I did graduate work on wolf issues at Isle Royale National Park, that being the reason for our stay in Wisconsin. But there are a number of things these kids don't know. Like that before they came along, dad was more of a hide-in-the-wilderness type than a stand-up-for-endangered-species guy. And like that their very presence helped galvanize a certain quit-hiding-and-start-standing-up-for-something mindset. And so finally, as the wolf issue arose in Colorado, dad was sitting there at his computer pecking away when the idea of "standing up" took on new meaning.

To be honest, I did not initially jump up and volunteer. Yes, I filled out the nomination form to be on the Wolf Working Group, but I let it set there on the edge of my desk for a month until the last day of consideration. Wolves are extremely political, to say the least, and I knew the stress level would be very high. My experience at Isle Royale taught me that wolves are an emotional, visceral topic, creatures for whom the plume of smoke circling in the air outsizes the fire on the ground by thousands of times. In the wolf reintroduction projects in the Northern Rockies and in New Mexico and Arizona, this chaos has only been amplified. People's opinions of wolves—for and against—flow at hurricane strength. And so I stared at the nomination form, wondering, "Why would I want to jump into that?"

But there it was, sitting on my desk, staring back, and for a solid month I played with the idea. What spurred me to action? No other creature has ever endured such vehement and totalitarian persecution as the United States wolf. They have been slaughtered, massacred, butchered, rounded up, ripped apart, desiccated, desecrated, blown to pieces, and poisoned by the hundreds of thousands (if not millions) so that finally, completely, they were uniformly eradicated and exterminated in the continental United States. What caused our blood to boil so hot? This surely says more about us, the predator, than the wolf, our prey.

Wolves are now officially endangered through an Act of Congress, and we have a very strong Colorado interest in recovering them and all endangered species. And so finally I stared at that form and I said, "If I can, I should stand up and help get a species removed from the endangered list, help right this terrible wrong. It would be useful and valuable work." I was trained, knowledgeable, and available, and if I couldn't stand up for a persecuted endangered species—a true *underdog*—then what the hell could I stand up for?

And as we drive through this chaotic postmodern scene here in the heart of Denver, our conversation in the car confirms to me that my stand-up-for-wolves decision was right. We talk a little more about wolves, and then our discussion turns back to the etchings along the interstate, which gradually change shape and form to resemble other critters and habitats. A strange conversation, indeed, to be having in a traffic jam on an interstate highway in a fast-growing American city. But there it is, nonetheless—we no longer curse the traffic, we no longer feel the heat and urban oppression. Instead, we wonder, we talk, we ask questions and we learn things about nature and each other. We enjoy. Nature, even in simulated form, draws us in and pulls us out. Instinct seems at work. Wildness beckons. Children's eyes widen, and then parents' eyes widen in return. I can't imagine what the hell else I ought to be doing. In my mind, the phrases "species extinction" and "wolf extermination" have no place on this earth. "Reintroduction" and "restoration" are the only credible choices.

The traffic jam finally eases up, and we quickly speed up to our normal seventy-mile-per-hour jaunt through south Denver. In a few moments we arrive in Dove Valley near the southern end (for now) of the ever-sprawling Denver metropolitan area, our destination for day's soccer tournament. As I look across the soccer complex—a twenty-acre irrigated bluegrass oasis—I see houses and strip malls marching east across the plains. But even here a kind of optimism and wildness lives.

As I walk around the soccer fields, a couple hundred young girls are either playing or warming up and a couple hundred more parents are sitting along the many sidelines. People yell out, "Go Fireballs," or "Way to go, Pumas." These are sounds I've heard a hundred times before, the nicknames we give our teams, evoking, I believe, a kind of wildness. While I wait for my daughter's game to start, I walk around and listen a bit more. I hear many nicknames—"Jaguars," "Pythons," and "Tornadoes." And strangely, a quarter-mile to the north sits the Denver "Broncos" headquarters, an orange and white monolithic building looming over the soccer complex.

Out on the soccer field I see a kind of wildness, too—girls screaming, running, and kicking. They knock each other around, knock each other down, and then they get right back up running and kicking again. They yell at each other as they race on and off the field, and they yell at each other all during the game. They are, after all, "Jaguars" and "Pythons" and "Tornadoes," wild and relentless with victory in their minds.

After my daughter's game ends, we slowly walk back to the van, making our way among the mass of parents, daughters, minivans, and SUVs. As we pass one field, I am again heartened at the possible future before us—a team of eight-year-old girls swirls in a huddle readying for their game, their hands piled high in the middle. In a shrieking cacophony, they recite a little cheer I've heard a hundred times over the past five years, yet they have a little twist at the end, a new, uncommon nickname:

We don't wear our mini-skirts
We just wear our soccer shirts.
We don't play with Barbie dolls
We just play with soccer balls.
Go, Go Gray Wolves!

And off they go, little gray wolves, running and screaming onto the field, our future alpha females of the human pack.

You might ask if this matters, this nicknaming, this image making, and it is a fair and honest question, for we have nicknamed ourselves many things over the years of our exterminating and extinguishing. I believe it does. I believe it helps us express what we wish to see and helps us speak for those who cannot speak; it is a kind of hope, perhaps, or a longing for wildness. What is an image, after all, but our attempt to imagine a different world?

Here in the heart of Denver and the surrounding suburbs, our imaginations are desperately needed to keep the wildness alive in the rest of Colorado. To have a healthy, sustainable population of wolves, we need our urban and suburban imaginations working in full force. We will need special license plates and cement interstate etchings, and many other images, groups, and tools—and yes, especially, money—to bring this different world about. We may even need bumper stickers that say, "Soccer Dads for Gray Wolves."

Tina Arapkiles

Tina Arapkiles is the southwest regional representative for the Sierra Club in Boulder, Colorado, and is codirector of the Southern Rockies Wolf Restoration Project. She has a degree in biology from the University of Colorado. In describing one of the stories she tells her children about wolves and other wild creatures, she speaks of the power of storytelling and her hope for the future.

Weaving Stories

We are camped at 11,500 feet above sea level beside a stream, engulfed by the glorious Colorado Rockies. It is our first backpacking trip into the wilderness with our girls—Nora, who is three, and Teelin, who is seven.

Rain pelted our tent all night; thunder and lightning echoed off the high cliff walls. I am tired from sleeplessness, but the girls slept through it all to awake refreshed and ready for another day of adventure.

They are happy in this natural state. Experienced campers, they find enjoyment within a twenty-foot radius of the tent, playing in the stream, making people with sticks and pinecones, hunting for mushrooms, rocks, and flowers. Our world—especially when we camp—is one of imagination, and of storytelling.

The stories we tell always have animals as the protagonists. People usually play a part, but almost always as secondary characters. Fairies and other magical characters sometimes find their way into the animals' adventures. I admit to anthropomorphizing animals in these stories. The bears are always curious and love berries. The owls, silent and nocturnal, are wise and protective of their young. The foxes are smart and constantly mischievous. The badger, determined and resourceful, is known for making perfect pie crust. Whales yearn for adventure and travel impossible distances to discover something new. Sea turtles, like wandering shamans of the vast ocean ecosystems, allow children to ride on their shells.

This morning a family of coyotes wakes to greet the sun at the same time my family emerges to start our morning camping routine. Nora, seeing an opportunity to begin a story, declares that the yips and yelps of the coyotes are those of wolves. She looks up at me, her hair in wild tangles. "Mama, would you tell a story about the wolves?" she asks. I look at Patrick and ask, "Do you mind?" He smiles, shakes his head, waves us away, and the three of us leave him to cook breakfast while we retreat into the tent to prepare for a story. We unzip the doors to let in fresh air and sunlight, and wrap ourselves into our still-warm sleeping bags.

"Teelin, you start," I say. She thinks for a minute and begins: "The wolf family wakes in the morning light. Your turn, Mama." I start to weave a story:

The papa and mama wolf had just come back to the rendezvous site with fresh meat to feed their family. The pups born this year were playing tag as the sunlight reached their den.

Automatically, the girls say, "Oh, how cute!"

They chased each other and rolled around in the tawny grass while the females in the pack looked on approvingly. This was a skillful litter.

They played so well together. They would be a successful family when the time came for them to be the leaders.

The pups born last year were not very patient with this year's litter. They had returned from the hunt and were discouraged. They kept up with their elders but were soundly rebuffed by the elk they had pursued. The oldest and most likely to become the alpha male swatted at the young pups and snarled, "Step aside. We're hungry."

"That wasn't very nice," says Nora.

After breakfast, the wolf family felt much better. The youngest puppies asked their mama and papa if they could go find their friends. Papa said, "Yes, but I want the older wolves to go with the puppies to keep an eye out for them. We don't want anyone drifting away in the current like yesterday!"

They all giggled, remembering the youngest puppy, still full of mischief, wandering into the camp all wet and cold after a float down the river.

The older ones helped the younger ones with their backpacks. They each packed a bottle of water, some food, an extra sweater, and a rain jacket.

As the puppies scampered off, their parents, aunts, and uncles watched with love in their hearts. They felt proud. Their young family was obedient.

They looked out for each other, learned from each other, and worked well together.

In the woods, the puppies met their friend the bear. Bear said, "Who wants to look for berries with me?" The youngest puppies, eager to play with their friend, all said, "I do!" The older wolves wandered off to practice catching voles. The wolf puppies and the bear went down the mountain, up a hill, over a creek, through a canyon, and up a south-facing slope to the biggest patch of raspberries in the region. They gathered and ate raspberries until their packs and their tummies were full of berries.

After a nice nap in the sun, they decided to visit their friend, the Old Lady, who lived alone in a cabin in the woods. She was kind to the forest animals and loved the wolf puppies. She had an orchard and a garden with vegetables that she shared with the rabbits and other vegetarians of the woods. Bear thought it was a good idea for them to share their raspberries with her since she was always sharing with the animals.

When they arrived, the Old Lady was sitting on her porch, drinking a cup of tea.

Just then, Patrick delivers our tea and oatmeal to the tent. He encourages us to come eat in the warm sunlight. As we crawl out, the coyote family yips and barks again. We look at each other with wide eyes. "They want you to keep telling the story, Mama," says Nora. We settle into the sunlight and our breakfast. I resume my story, pausing every now and then to soak up the scenery, bask in the solitude, and remark upon our good fortune of health and family.

The Old Lady was so glad to see the puppies and Bear! The puppies jumped in her lap and licked her face as she squealed with delight, "You've been eating raspberries!" After they all calmed down and showed her the berries, the Old Lady said, "Let's call Badger over to make crust for raspberry tarts!" They all knew that Badger made the best piecrust around. Bear bounded away to retrieve Badger for a day in the Old Lady's kitchen.

The story goes on and on. We add pieces and forget parts when we retell it. The girls participate at times but mostly, these days, I'm the storyteller.

On this day, as the sun rises in the clear blue sky, the story ends with the wolf pups bringing raspberry tarts to their family. The pups were proud to provide food for the family just like their papa and mama.

Teelin asks, "Mama, those weren't really wolves we heard this morning, were they?" She knows I've been working to get wolves reintroduced into the Southern Rockies since she was born.

I say, "No, they were coyotes."

Nora asks, "Will we hear wolves someday when we camp?" I gaze at the beauty around me and wonder.

I reply to my children, "I sure hope so."

Hal Clifford

Hal Clifford is the executive editor of Orion *magazine and author of three books about the Colorado mountains, including* Downhill Slide: Why the Corporate Ski Industry is Bad for Skiing, Ski Towns, and the Environment. *"Saved by Wolves" summarizes much of what motivates those who would return wolves to their former homes, a restoration, he says, that might allow us to "stitch ourselves into the fabric of place."*

Saved by Wolves

For people like me who have defined our destiny by looking and going West (in other words, for generations of Americans), Interstate 70 makes perfect sense. But one winter day in the late 1990s, while researching a book about the ills of the modern ski industry, I gazed down from the slopes of Beaver Creek ski area at the double ribbon of pavement snaking through the Eagle River valley and I thought about a newspaper headline that suggested the road made no sense at all: "I-70 Like Berlin Wall for Wildlife, Biologists Say." At the time, I was considering the elk that were being crowded north by the resort and had to run the deadly gauntlet of the highway. Not long after, though, and not far away, something very different encountered that same "wall" trying to come south. On June 7, 2004, a two-year-old female gray wolf turned up dead along the side of Interstate 70. The wolf, apparently killed by a speeding vehicle as she tried to cross the four lanes west of Idaho Springs, was simply doing what wolves do. She'd left her Yellowstone pack in January and headed south, seeking terrain, food, a mate. Her demise was an individual tragedy, but it represents hope for a species. Hope for wolves, yes, but the species I have in mind is human beings.

There was an era, its center of gravity situated in the 1950s, when many Americans felt that our future would be one of technological triumph over the vicissitudes of messy, inefficient nature. In this naive, halcyon time, we were as close in our minds to the world represented by Buck Rogers and

George Jetson as we likely ever will be. But the future turned out to be a good deal more unmanageable and complex than Madison Avenue promised during the Eisenhower administration. We live, as a consequence, in a frightening time, and it's hard to make sense of it. Much of what passes for news in the mass media dwells upon the Hobbesian elements of our present circumstances, the distracting but meaningless (at least to the larger society) car crashes and homicidal rampages; the perpetual war; the plucky child overcoming some bitter sentence dished up by fate. But there are other refractions from this world's faceted complexity, less likely to end up on the ten o'clock news but infinitely more worthy of our attention, and these cause me to be thrilled to be alive in this age of rediscovery—after all, the Enlightenment was terrifying, too, at least when viewed from the cheap seats.

It is probably impossible to understand the import of events, in particular those that shift the direction of history, while they are under way. Only in hindsight does what happened become clear. But I believe we are experiencing an extraordinary awakening. Beginning with the writings of Aldo Leopold and Rachel Carson, Americans slowly have embraced the complexity of the world. We have come to understand the ideas of ecology and ecosystems, and to see the wisdom in Leopold's rephrasing of God's instructions to Noah when he wrote that "the first rule of intelligent tinkering is to keep all the pieces." Pieces, species—we've got a pretty good grip by now on what he and He were talking about.

"Ecology," said Barry Lopez, "is the study of the coherence of community." Our understanding of ecology has informed our understanding of the larger world. We have come to see on the geopolitical level that relationships matter. A lot. We have come to see on the molecular level that subatomic particles are defined by their relationships. We have learned that the genetic map of a genome turns out to be little more than a rough sketch of the profoundly mysterious skein of relationships between genes and the individuals they shape. We have come to embrace chaos theory, to understand—albeit very imperfectly—that the wings of a butterfly can, indeed, generate a hurricane. I use the term "we" advisedly, for I know that I'm writing about only a portion of America, a portion of the world. I know that even as millions of people are embracing this newly visible complexity, millions more are pulling back into a hard place ramparted by human constructions of value. Theirs is a world of Manichean distinctions: man and nature, good and evil, black and white. I understand the impulse; I, too, am terrified on a daily basis by the entropy around me. In an increasingly complex world, simplicity has great appeal.

Among the simple ideas that shaped America was this: The land was put here by God for us (that is, recent immigrants) to use for human benefit. So those things that stood in our way—native peoples, wolves and bears, droughts and mountains—we overcame. This approach lent itself admirably to the creation of powerful national myths of conquest. We grew on *Bonanza* and *Shane* and *The Rifleman,* and we liked what their comfortable parables told us: There was right and wrong, livestock and varmints, crops and weeds, and it was both easy to tell the difference and moral to act upon it. Lately, facts have been intruding on these nice stories, as they are wont to do. Drought, for instance—the sort of drought the West has seen before, albeit not for a long time—is reshaping the landscape. Yet still in the West there is a powerful, fundamentalist strain that battles nature—and what better foe than the big bad wolf?—that fails to see that when man acts against nature he acts against himself. It is a fight, and the language and symbolism, from the violence of children's games of cowboys-and-Indians to the modern rodeo, is about that fighting. But nature is saying—not only in the dusty flanks of Lake Powell, but also in the tracks of a lone wolf that came sniffing down through Colorado not long ago—that I am here to be reckoned with on my own terms, and that you, Man, are part of me. You and I, we have a relationship.

And so enter the lone gray wolf, harbinger of its kind. What are we to make of this? How are we to respond to it? The wolf is no harmless songbird. Even before the fabulist Brothers Grimm put quill to paper, the wolf has been persecuted in our culture's art and literature. Lately it has been reformed in some circles, championed as charismatic megafauna worthy of calendar art. We define and redefine the wolf, yet who owns the wolf? The question seems absurd, like asking who owns the wind or the river. Before the United States existed, the peoples who inhabited the American land didn't even recognize the idea of land ownership. The wolf existed on its own terms, for its own reasons, as all things did. That era is long gone, though, replaced by one in which we have not only private property rights (including the right to use the wind's power and the river's water), but also the Clean Air Act and Clean Water Act. And so the question must be asked and answered: All of us own the wolf, just as all of us own the air we breathe and the water we drink. We depend on the air and water, of course. But we depend on the wolf, too, and we have a need to defend the wolf as we defend the air and water—for our own good, not simply for the wolf's.

Scholars have suggested that humans did not domesticate the wolf; the wolf may have chosen humans as a companion and hunting mate, setting the genus *Lupus* on a course that culminated in the Westminster Dog Show. We and wolves enjoy the oldest of human-animal relationships, and it is mined with the pitfalls of vestigial memory. The wolf is not a simple thing—not in its needs or expressions, nor in its relationship to human culture. And so, again, how are we to react to its return to Colorado? The tide of history and our expanding knowledge offer only one honest and self-serving option: Embrace the complexity the wolf represents. The wolf is good for human beings, and not simply in a squishy, feel-good way. When I consider the wolf I see the expression of a full web of life, from the nematodes to the fungus to the vole, from the vulture to the pine beetle to the mule deer, all there in a dark and elusive form on four swift paws. The wolf's thriving signals that much is right with the broader world upon which it depends. Unbalanced ecosystems—signaled to us by landscapes absent wolves, by poisoned topsoil on industrial farms, by estuarine dead zones killed by runoff, by lakes sterile from acid rainfall—are more than biological tragedies. They are human tragedies, too. Such failures of our collective imagination and will (which is what pollution and land degradation represent) cost jobs, lives, and cold hard cash.

We are not wise enough to understand what in nature, if anything, is expendable. There was a time less than a century ago when a conservationist as thoughtful as Aldo Leopold embraced the idea that eliminating predators would help deer populations in northern Arizona. The result was a nightmare—not only for the predators (including wolves), which were hunted ruthlessly, but for the deer and the forests upon which they depended. The deer quickly overpopulated their range, stripping the land of anything remotely edible, then died en masse of starvation. The less we understand (and we understand little), the more we must embrace the precautionary, quasi-religious strategy of proceeding with humility. We must keep all the parts. The act of doing so is our best insurance that nature—including us first and foremost—will thrive.

Beneath this practical argument lies a moral one: Nature is intrinsically valuable. We are told this through our religious texts (Noah's story is among the first we learn); through numberless scientific studies; and through what the biologist E. O. Wilson has called our innate "biophilia," or love of all things living. We depend on life. All life depends on life.

I have often envied the American men and women, including my father's father, who fought World War II and rebuilt the world in its aftermath—not for their battlefield heroics or home-front privations, but for their vision and sense of the possible. They had saved the world, after all. In the quiet years following the war they lived, perhaps more than any other generation, in an era of seemingly unlimited possibility. There was a can-do quality about them, and so they built the great dams and highways of the West, threw up cities in the desert, flew higher and faster than ever before.

There is irony inherent to this envy—after all, what I've just described is the very hubris that got us into many of the messes we suffer today, and I put pen to paper now to advocate for humility. But that irony aside, who has the vision today that they did then? Who would imagine seeing such possibilities, much less realizing them? We live in a time of fear, of getting by, keeping our heads down, and hoping for the best. Our expansive, inclusive national vision seems to have disintegrated into a landscape of gated communities, defensive driving, cultural balkanization, and mutual suspicion.

But I continue to think we live also in a hopeful time, and that the defining chance for greatness has been laid at our doorstep. I spent twenty years in the mountains of Colorado and of course never heard a wolf—never imagined that I could. That roadkilled wolf on the side of I-70 has cracked open a kernel of possibility, and not just because I want to hear wolf songs in the Elks and the West Elks, the Collegiates and San Juans and Sangre de Cristos. I thrill at the idea of the wolf because it is a beckoning thing. Come, says the wolf. I am the totem of your calling.

My grandfather and his generation rebuilt the world as their era needed it to be. Now, we must rebuild it again, as we need it to be, not as the world of black-and-white separateness upon which so much American myth has been piled. Wallace Stegner hoped that the West would develop "a society to match its scenery." But Stegner had it wrong. The society and scenery are the same thing in the American West, indeed the American nation. The sooner we understand that, the sooner we will recognize that the wholeness of the land is the root upon which the richness of the people feeds. This is the renaissance of the land. The wolf sings it into being. The wolf is all the connections of the land, and that includes our connection, too. As we make room for the wolf we take another step toward embracing the complexity of the world—the glorious, magical complexity that is the expression of God in all things—and we begin to stitch ourselves into the fabric of place.

Veronica Patterson

Veronica Patterson, who lives in Loveland, won the Colorado Book Award for her poetry collection Swan, What Shores? *She was also for many years codirector of Loveland's "Poets in the Park" annual event. Her poem here offers powerful last words for this collection, as she imagines a landscape made whole by wolves and speaks movingly of all the things their presence might "begin to mend"—"holes / in the web? absences in the landscape? we?"*

Landscape with Wolves

Every pine cuts the shape of a wolf,
sitting on its haunches, its nose
raised to the sky, silently howling.
—Kathleen Dean Moore, "Howling with Strangers"

In the mountains, I find a faint track
they might follow. Where light and dark
play on canyon walls, I sense swift shapes
in shadow. Tawny hills suggest belly fur.
Below a hollowed bank, in fitful wind,
bushes jostle like pups.
As always, aspen spend their thin coins
on earth. Only pines are silhouetted
on the ridge the sun slips down. But
when the moon lifts above peaks, I listen
for a howl, hear one voice, then another,
echo up a ravine toward snowfields.
Could these cords of sound ripple
through a torn web of being
and begin slow repairs? We
invite wolves, and something—holes
in the web? absences in the landscape? we?
begin to mend.

Resources

Historic and Current Range
of the Gray Wolf in the United States

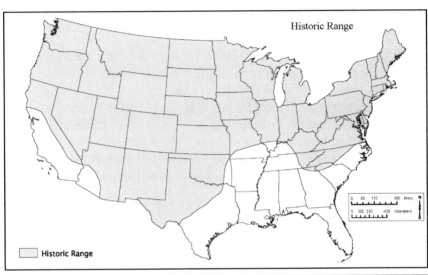

Historic Range

Historic Range

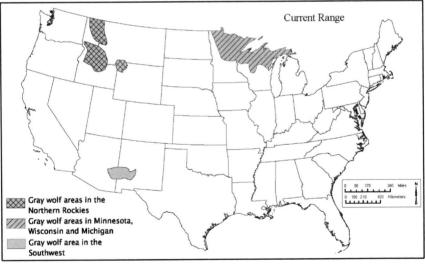

Current Range

Gray wolf areas in the Northern Rockies

Gray wolf areas in Minnesota, Wisconsin and Michigan

Gray wolf area in the Southwest

Defenders of Wildlife: The Bailey Wildlife Foundation Proactive Carnivore Conservation Fund

Wolves, grizzly bears and other predators are slowly reclaiming parts of their former ranges in the lower forty-eight states and elsewhere in North America. Occasionally, these carnivores may prey on livestock or cause other problems. Defenders of Wildlife believes that the same public that seeks more room for predators has a responsibility to help resolve conflicts associated with the recovery of these animals.

Working with landowners, resource managers, and others to prevent or reduce predator problems has important conservation benefits. Human-caused mortality, including illegal killings and lethal control by government agencies in response to livestock predation incidents, remains the single leading cause of wolf mortality in the northern Rockies and the American Southwest. Similarly, about one-third of grizzly bear deaths each year are attributable to government control actions in response to conflicts on private lands.

Defenders created the Proactive Carnivore Conservation Fund to prevent conflict between imperiled predators and humans before it occurs. The fund was renamed The Bailey Wildlife Foundation Proactive Carnivore Conservation Fund in recognition for the foundation's generous gift. It is a natural outgrowth of our wolf and grizzly compensation programs. If landowners or other entities have repeated predator problems, we ask them to propose projects that will help reduce conflict. If the concept is practical and within our means, we share the cost of the project. Projects can also be proposed by government agencies or by Defenders.

This proactive fund has three objectives: (1) to reduce conflicts between predators and humans; (2) to keep predators from being unnecessarily killed by agencies in response to human conflicts; and (3) to increase general tolerance for carnivores across the landscape. We believe that our success at expanding the range of predators across the American West and elsewhere will be directly proportional to our success at reducing conflict between predators and humans.

Defenders' proactive program was initiated in Montana, Idaho, Wyoming, Arizona, and New Mexico, but it is expanding to address conflicts in select areas across North America, including Colorado. Proposed projects are prioritized based on the level of human-carnivore conflict in the area and the likelihood that the proposed solution will resolve the problem.

For more information, please contact: Defenders of Wildlife, 1130 17th Street NW, Washington, DC   20036; (202) 682-9400; info@defenders.org; http://www.defenders.org/wildlife/new/facts/pro.html.

The Rewilding Institute:
A North American Wolf Vision

In 1600, wolves lived in North America from the high Arctic islands to just north of the Valley of Mexico, and from the Atlantic to Pacific. Beginning with the earliest European settlements, colonists declared war against wolves. By the middle of the twentieth century, wolves were essentially extirpated from the United States and Mexico.

We now know that the fear of wolves was based on myths, and that wolves are a vital and necessary part of healthy, functioning North American ecosystems. With this new knowledge, tentative efforts have been made to restore wolves in the most out-of-the-way parts of temperate North America.

However, these restoration efforts by the US Fish and Wildlife Service endeavor only to recover small, geographically isolated populations encompassing a relatively insignificant proportion of their historic range. Furthermore, the USFWS has no plans for restoring wolves to substantial areas of potentially suitable habitat (the Southern Rocky Mountains, New England, and the Pacific Northwest, for example).

We call for the recovery of wolves across North America. Such recovery means:

- Restoration of wolves in suitable habitat throughout their former range in North America, from the Northern Sierra Madre Occidental in Mexico to the Canadian Rockies and Coast Range, and from the U.S. Pacific Northwest to the Upper Great Lakes and to upstate New York and New England.

- Restoration of potentially suitable habitats and crucial linkages between patches of suitable wolf habitat where wolves are free to behave like wolves.

- Restoration of wolves in ecologically and evolutionarily effective populations so that they may fulfill their natural keystone role of ecosystem regulation, aiding the persistence of native flora and fauna.

- Restoration of wolves throughout this expanse, so that all wolf populations are connected by a continuum of functioning dispersal linkages.

In short, we envision the return of the wolf to its rightful place in North American wildlands, to a community where humans dwell with respect and tolerance for wild species.

(As of this book's publication date, this Vision has been endorsed by the Sierra Club, Arizona Wilderness Coalition, Grand Canyon Wildlands Council, Sinapu, Center for Biological Diversity, and the Wildlands Project. Organizations or individuals interested in endorsing this vision can contact The Rewilding Institute, PO Box 13768, Albuquerque, NM 87192.)

Organizations Promoting
Wolf Recovery in the Mountain West

Colorado and the Southern Rockies

Sinapu
1911 11th Street, Suite 103
Boulder, CO 80302
(303) 447-8655
www.sinapu.org

Southern Rockies Wolf Restoration Project
www.rockywolf.org

Southwest

Arizona Wilderness Coalition
PO Box 529
Alpine, AZ 85920
(928) 339-4426
www.azwild.org

Grand Canyon Wildlands
PO Box 1594
Flagstaff, Arizona 86002
(928) 556-9306
www.grandcanyonwildlands.org

New Mexico Wilderness Alliance
202 Central SE Suite 101
Albuquerque, NM 87102
(505) 843-8696
www.nmwild.org

Center for Biological Diversity
PO Box 710
Tucson, AZ 85702–0710
(520) 623-5252
www.sw-center.org

Utah

Utah Wolf Forum
www.utahwolf.net

Northern Rockies

Alliance for Wild Rockies
PO Box 8731
Missoula, MT 59807
(406) 721-5420
www.wildrockiesalliance.org

Predator Conservation Alliance
PO Box 6733
Bozeman, MT 59771
(406) 587-3389
www.predatorconservation.org

Wolf Recovery Foundation
P.O. Box 444
Pocatello, ID 83204
http://forwolves.org

National

Defenders of Wildlife
1130 17th Street, NW
Washington, DC 20036
(202) 682-9400
www.defenders.org

International Wolf Center
1396 Highway 169
Ely, Minnesota 55731–8129
(800) 359-9653
www.wolf.org

National Wildlife Federation
1400 16th Street NW
Washington DC 20036
(202) 797-6800
www.nwf.org

The Rewilding Institute
PO Box 13768
Albuquerque, NM 87192
www.rewilding.org

Sierra Club
85 Second Street, 2nd Floor
San Francisco, CA 94105
(415) 977-5500
www.sierraclub.org

Turner Endangered Species Fund
1123 Research Drive
Bozeman MT 59718
(406) 556-8500
www.tesf.org

The Wildlands Project
PO Box 455
Richmond, VT 05477
(802) 434-4077
www.twp.org

Links to USFWS Recovery Efforts

USFWS Region 6 Gray Wolf News
http://westerngraywolf.fws.gov

USFWS Midwest Gray Wolf Site
http://www.fws.gov/midwest/wolf/

USFWS Mexican Wolf Recovery Site
http://ifw2es.fws.gov/mexicanwolf/

For Further Reading

Rick Bass, *The Ninemile Wolves* (Houghton Mifflin, 1992)

Charles Bergman, *Wild Echoes: Encounters with the Most Endangered Animals in North America* (McGraw-Hill, 1990; University of Illinois Press, 2003)

David E. Brown, ed., *The Wolf in the Southwest: The Making of an Endangered Species* (University of Arizona Press, 1984)

Robert Busch, *The Wolf Almanac* (Lyons Press, 1998)

Roger A. Caras, *The Custer Wolf: Biography of an American Renegade* (Little, Brown, 1966; University of Nebraska Press, 1990)

Tim W. Clark, A. Peyton Curlee, Steven C. Minta, and Peter M. Kareiva, eds., *Carnivores in Ecosystems: The Yellowstone Experience* (Yale University Press, 1999)

Roberta L. Hall and Henry S. Sharp, *Wolf and Man: Evolution in Parallel* (Academic Press, 1978)

Jim Harrison, *Wolf: A False Memoir* (Houghton Mifflin, 1971)

R. D. Lawrence, *The Green Hills Beyond: A Memoir* (Henry Holt, 1994)

Aldo Leopold, *A Sand County Almanac* (Oxford University Press, 1949)

Jack London, *The Call of the Wild* (Simon & Schuster, 1994)

Barry Lopez, *Of Wolves and Men* (Scribners, 1978)

Rick McIntyre, *War Against the Wolf: America's Campaign to Exterminate the Wolf* (Voyageur Press, 1995)

Thomas McNamee, *The Return of the Wolf to Yellowstone* (Henry Holt, 1997)

L. David Mech, *The Wolf: The Ecology and Behavior of an Endangered Species* (University of Minnesota Press, 1981)

L. David Mech and Luigi Boitani, eds., *Wolves: Behavior, Ecology, and Conservation* (University of Chicago Press, 2003)

Farley Mowat, *Never Cry Wolf* (Little, Brown, 1963; Back Bay Books, 2001)

Adolph Murie, *The Wolves of Mount McKinley* (U.S. Government Printing Office, 1944; University of Washington Press, 1985)

Peter Steinhart, *The Company of Wolves* (Alfred A. Knopf, 1995)

Art Wolfe and Gregory McNamee, *In the Presence of Wolves* (Crown Publishers, 1995)